More
ALL-TIME
HOCKEY LISTS

More ALL-TIME HOCKEY LISTS

STAN AND SHIRLEY FISCHLER

McGraw-Hill Ryerson

Toronto • Montreal

Copyright © 1994 Stan Fischler

All rights reserved. No part of this publication may be reproduced or transmitted in any form or by any means, or stored in a data base and retrieval system, without the prior written permission of the publisher.

First published in 1994 by
McGraw-Hill Ryerson Ltd.
300 Water Street
Whitby, Ontario, Canada
L1N 9B6

Publisher: Donald S. Broad

Canadian Cataloguing in Publication Data

Fischler, Stan, 1932-
    More hockey lists

ISBN 0-07-551821-X

1. Hockey - Miscellanea. 2. National Hockey League - Miscellanea. 3. Hockey - Anecdotes. I. Fischler, Shirley. II. Title

GV847.F57 1994   796.962   C94-932430-3

Cover design: Dave Hader/Studio Conceptions
Text design: Jacqueline Lealess
Editorial services provided by Word Guild, Toronto

This book was produced for McGraw-Hill Ryerson by Shaftesbury Books, a member of the Warwick Publishing Group, Toronto.

Printed and bound in Canada

Dedication

One of our most treasured lists consists of those in the hockey community who rallied to our side when our son, Simon, was stricken with cardiomyopathy in June 1993. The support was super and helped Simon through his crisis.

Since the list would encompass too many pages, we'll simply say that this book is dedicated to the Hockey Community.

Acknowledgements

No book of lists would be complete without a list of those who made it possible.

Our thanks to Stephanie Toskos, Dave Levy, Nicole Salomone, Dave Kolb, and Reverend Glen R. Goodhand.

Table of Contents

The Six Reasons Why the Rangers Were Able To Win the Stanley Cup After 54 Years and a Dozen Curses • 1
Three Places that Prove Canadians No Longer Own Hockey • 2
The Two Coaches Who Proved that It Doesn't Pay To Be a Stanley Cup-Winner • 3
The Two Best Quotes from the Fred Shero Family • 4
Late Maple Leafs Owner Harold Ballard's Two Most Pungent Putdowns of His Stylish But Non-Belligerent European Forward Inge Hammarstrom • 4
Two Best Female Entertainers at NHL Games • 5
The Three Most Absurd Rinks in the NHL • 6
Best Headline for a Silly Story About a Czech Hockey Player • 6
The Three Best Books About the Esposito Family • 7
Longest Delay in Learning About Being Traded • 8
Boom Boom Geoffrion's Two Favorite Rocket Richard Stories • 8
Gordie Howe's Two Favorite Moments • 10
Bobby Hull's Proudest Moment • 11
Dennis Hull's Two Biggest Thrills • 11
Dennis Hull's Favorite Putdown of Himself • 12
Dennis Hull's Two Favorite Putdowns of San Jose Sharks Rookie Pat Falloon When Hull Was a TV Analyst • 12
Dennis Hull's Two Other Favorite Quips While Broadcasting in the San Francisco Bay Area • 13
Jacques Demers' Most Inspirational Eight Words • 13
Strangest Reason To Fire a Good Coach • 13
Four Women Who Broke the All-Male Public Relations Barrier in the NHL • 14
Glenn Anderson's Two Flakiest Moments • 15
Jaromir Jagr's Two Favorite Department Store Capers • 16

Jacques Demers' Two Most Embarrassing Moments as a Coach • 17
Referee Paul Stewart's Best On-Ice Putdowns • 18
Three Cherished Assets of Chicago Stadium to be Mourned in its Passing • 18
Name the Only Retired Professional Soccer Player, Professional Musician and Linguist who is a Premier NHL Ice-Maker • 19
Gump Worsley's Two Best Wisecracks • 20
Three Reasons Why Gordie Howe Will Always Rank Above Wayne Gretzky on the All-Time List of Great Scorers • 20
Two Significant Women Who Have Been Involved in Men's Hockey • 21
Ten Most Appropriate Names • 22
Ten Unusual Birthplaces • 24
Seven Countries You'd Never Expect to Produce NHL Players • 25
The Three Most Misspelled Names • 26
The Top Ten by Nations • 27
The Three Best — and Last — Players To Wear Regular Glasses in the NHL • 34
The Five Best Mayhem-Inspiring Names • 35
Four Reasons Why the Winnipeg Jets Were Draft Disasters • 35
The First Player Ever Drafted Twice • 36
The Worst Case of Foot-In-Draft Disease, as Recorded by Terry Crisp • 37
The Ten Best Hockey Stories of the '30s and '40s, as Told By Hall-of-Fame Goalie Chuck Rayner • 37
The Two Best Rats in Hockey History • 49
Six Zanies on Ice and Their Stunts • 50
The Three Best Lines With Nicknames • 52
The Ten Craziest Non-1994 Encounters of the Stanley Cup • 54
The Ten Craziest 1994 Encounters of the Stanley Cup • 56
Hall-of-Fame Goalie Glenn Hall's Seven Memorable Moments • 58

FOUR REASONS WHY ALEXANDER DAIGLE IS THE BIGGEST BUILD-UP
    TO A LETDOWN OF THE 1990S • 62
FOUR PEOPLE WHO WOULD RATHER VISIT LOWER SLOBOVIA THAN
    UPPER QUEBEC CITY • 63
THE BIGGEST TOP DRAFT PICK-FLOP TO BECOME A PLAYERS' AGENT
    • 63
THE THREE MOST SIGNIFICANT PLAYERS' STRIKES • 64
THE BEST AND WORST OF BRIAN SUTTER AS COACH • 67
FROM THE PENTHOUSE TO THE OUTHOUSE TO THE BROADCAST
    BOOTH • 67
GLEN SONMOR'S FAVORITE BILL GOLDTHORPE STORY • 68
MOST HONEST ADMISSION OF FIBBERY BY AN NHL COACH • 69
GARY BETTMAN'S TEN BEST MOVES SINCE BECOMING COMMISSIONER
    • 69
FIVE MISTAKES BY BETTMAN • 72
THE FIVE BEST WATSONS • 72
THE TWO BEST CAT GOALTENDERS • 74
THE TEN BEST HOCKEY CENTERS IN NORTH AMERICA • 75
NATIONAL HOCKEY LEAGUE PLAYERS WHO HAVE BEEN NAMED TO
    THE ORDER OF CANADA • 77
THE THREE MOST RELEVANT CONTEMPORARY HOCKEY PEOPLE
    WHOSE NAMES BEGIN WITH THE LETTER G • 78
THE TEN BEST FIGHTERS OF THE PAST DECADE • 79
THE RECORD FOR HOME GAMES PLAYED ON THE ROAD BY A PRO
    TEAM • 81
BEST NHL PLAY-BY-PLAY MAN AS THESPIAN • 81
THE TWO WORST NHL ROOF COLLAPSES • 82
BEST ONE-EYED PERSONALITIES • 83
MOST EMBARRASSING DEBUT FOR A HOCKEY TEAM • 83
FIVE REASONS WHY GIL STEIN HAD THE SHORTEST TERM OF ANY
    NATIONAL HOCKEY LEAGUE PRESIDENT • 84
THE GREATEST LINE NOT IN THE NHL • 84
BEST PUTDOWN OF A WAYNE GRETZKY-OWNED AUTOMOBILE • 86
TOP SIX PLAYERS PLAYOFF TEAMS CAN'T AFFORD TO LOSE • 86
TOP FIVE POWER FORWARDS • 87

Best Franchise Players at Each Position • 88
Three Gutsy Moves by Injured Players • 90
The Absolutely Worst Use of a Curved Stick in Playoff Annals • 92
Most Interesting U-Turn on a Hockey Autobiography • 93
The Six Best Conachers in Hockey • 93
Most Unusual Probe of a Hockey Fan's Car • 95
Most Unusual Place for a Hockey Fan to Propose Marriage • 96
Best Press Room Fight in Canada, 1993-94 • 96
Rocket Richard's Favorite Goal • 96
Three Reasons Why Pat Burns Won't Win A Stanley Cup With the Leafs • 98
Five Reasons Why Hockey Officiating is the Worst of All Major Sports • 98
Hollywood's Best Hockey Movies • 98
The All Time Non-NHL Losers • 102
The Most Traded Man In Hockey • 105
The Worst Team Ever • 108

The Six Reasons Why the Rangers Were Able To Win the Stanley Cup After 54 Years and a Dozen Curses

1. *The Law of Averages*: Sooner or later, The Law catches up with everyone and every team. After five decades and six different National Hockey League presidents, even the Rangers were due.

2. *Money:* Then owned by Paramount Communications, the Rangers had the richest organization in the league. They were able to nab big stars such as Mark Messier and solid second-liners like Esa Tikkanen that other clubs couldn't afford. By constantly dealing with the cash-poor Edmonton Oilers, the New Yorkers spent millions for stars.

3. *Fading Curses:* Former New York Americans owner Red Dutton was angry at the Rangers for forcing his club out of business. Dutton reportedly claimed that the Rangers would never win the Stanley Cup as long as he was alive. Alas, The Redhead died on March 15, 1987. Even then, The Curse lasted seven years.

4. *Luck:* The Rangers had the extreme good fortune of encountering a reeling Islanders team in the first playoff round and an injury-riddled Capitals club in the second round. Against the Devils, no less than two sudden-death goals by Stephane Matteau were flukes, including the Cup-winner which went in off goalie Martin Brodeur's back.

5. *Mike Keenan:* In a stroke of motivational genius, the new coach produced a tape of the kind of Broadway victory

parade the Rangers would have if they won the Cup. It was shown in training camp, and Keenan kept his troops hypnotized 'til the end.

6. *Mark Messier:* With his team down three-games-to-two to the New Jersey Devils, the Rangers captain vowed publically that New York would win Game Six. Messier made good on his promise by scoring a hat trick, ensuring victory after the Rangers had been down 2-0.

THREE PLACES THAT PROVE CANADIANS NO LONGER OWN HOCKEY

1. *Tampa Bay, Florida:* In the months before the Lightning received an NHL franchise, it was freely predicted that there were too many old people in this community and too few hockey fans. Since then, the Lightning have set an all-time league attendance record at The Thunderdome with many crowds in excess of 20,000. That's more than the biggest audience at The Forum, Maple Leaf Gardens and Winnipeg Arena, where hockey is king.

2. *Anaheim, California:* Lord Stanley of Preston must have turned over in his grave when an NHL club was named The Mighty Ducks. Yet here was a brand-new team, playing right in the shadow of Wayne Gretzky and the Los Angeles Kings and in its maiden season, 1993-94, sold out most games.

3. *Miami, Florida:* On the final night of the 1993-94 season the first-year Florida Panthers — already eliminated from the playoffs — played an insignificant game against the New York Islanders. Not only did the game sell out, but

the crowd roared as if the home club was a dynasty. "I thought by their noise," said Bill Torrey, the Panthers President, "that we were about to win the Stanley Cup."

A Stanley Cup champion coach in 1938, Bill Stewart was rapidly fired by Blackhawks owner Frederic McLaughlin that same year. Stewart didn't have to look far to get work: he doubled as a major league baseball umpire.

THE TWO COACHES WHO PROVED THAT IT DOESN'T PAY TO BE A STANLEY CUP-WINNER

1. *Bill Stewart.* The grandfather of NHL referee Paul Stewart, Bill was a major league baseball umpire as well as NHL referee. But in the 1937-38 season he performed the near-impossible. Stewart took a Chicago Blackhawks club which finished with a 14-25-9 record and directed them to the Stanley Cup. Hawks owner Major Frederic McLaughlin rewarded Stewart for his efforts by firing him only 21 games into the new season, although Chicago had a much better record than in the Cup-winning year.

2. *Al MacNeil.* In 1970-71 the Montreal Canadiens, with a just-average club, were pumped to a 31-15-9 record under MacNeil. The Maritimer then orchestrated one of the greatest upsets of all time — the Habs over Bobby Orr and the Big, Bad Bruins — in the opening playoff round followed by triumphs over Minnesota and Chicago for the Stanley Cup. But during the finals captain Henri (Pocket Rocket) Richard called MacNeil "the worst coach I ever played for" and — poof! just like that — MacNeil was gone before the next season began.

THE TWO BEST QUOTES FROM THE FRED SHERO FAMILY

1. "Take the shortest distance to the puck, and arrive in ill-humor." —*Fred Shero, while coaching the Philadelphia Flyers, a.k.a. The Broad Street Bullies.*

2. "If you could open up his head, I think you'd find a little rink inside." —*Mrs. Fred Shero*

LATE MAPLE LEAFS OWNER HAROLD BALLARD'S TWO MOST PUNGENT PUTDOWNS OF HIS STYLISH BUT NON-BELLIGERENT EUROPEAN FORWARD INGE HAMMARSTROM

1. "He could go into the corner with eggs in his pockets, and come out with none of them broken."

2. "Chicken Swede!"

Two Best Female Entertainers at NHL Games

1. *Kate Smith.* One of America's greatest popular vocalists, Smith was invited to a Philadelphia Flyers game at The Spectrum to sing her signature tune, "God Bless America." The Flyers won that night, so owner Ed Snider invited her back two more times in the 1970s and Philadelphia won all three games, including a 1-0 Stanley Cup-winner over Boston on May 19, 1974. The Flyers then began playing recordings of Smith's rendition of "God Bless America." After 78 games, their record was 62-13-3. Following Kate's death on June 17, 1986, the organization erected a statue of Smith outside the arena.

2. *Gladys Goodding.* An excellent popular organist, Goodding became the house entertainer at New York Rangers games at Madison Square Garden during the 1940s. (She also played for Brooklyn Dodgers baseball games and New York Knicks basketball games. Hence, the trivia queston, "Who played for the Rangers, Knicks and Dodgers?") Gladys would play a tune for each NHL club when it skated on to the ice, such as "Pretty Red Wing" for Detroit and "Chicago, Chicago" for the Blackhawks. And she never missed a "Happy Birthday" when it was required. Miss Goodding also had the most misspelled name in sports; editors always thought the extra D was a mistake. Which it wasn't.

The Three Most Absurd Rinks in the NHL

1. *The Thunderdome in St. Petersburg, Florida.* This is a baseball park masquerading as a hockey arena. It got that way when the city fathers failed to lure a major league baseball team to the white elephant it had constructed just for that purpose. Though the crowds have been big, hockey in a baseball yard just doesn't work. Fortunately, a new arena is under construction in downtown Tampa.

2. *The Aud in Buffalo.* Not only is the rink undersized, but so are the rest of the facilities. The visiting team's dressing rooms are so small that the players would be better off dressing at their hotels and just bussing straight to the bench.

3. *Madison Square Garden.* How can any self-respecting team call a perfectly round building square? Never mind that; the arena was obsolete the night it opened in 1968. A few years ago $300 million was spent to renovate the mess but MSG remains a formica-looking monstrosity with the worst sightlines for the highest-priced tickets in hockey.

Best Headline for a Silly Story About a Czech Hockey Player

"REMEMBER, ROMAN WASN'T BUILT IN A DAY." The headline appeared over a story in *The Tampa Tribune* by Martin Fennelly. The author tells about the time Czechoslovak-born defenseman Roman Hamrlik bought a fancy Mitsubishi 3000 and brought it to practice. "It was a beautiful thing," recalls then-Lightning defenseman Rob

Ramage. "It came right from the showroom. After practice, I come out and there's Roman and his dad, just sitting in the car, enjoying it. Then I realize they're sitting there because Roman doesn't know how to start it. I guess they showed him once at the dealership, and he got it to practice, but that was it. Just sat there. So I started it for him. That sums up the first NHL year for Roman — a little lost!"

THE THREE BEST BOOKS ABOUT THE ESPOSITO FAMILY

1. *HOCKEY IS MY LIFE* (Dodd, Mead) By Phil Esposito with Gerry Eskenazi. Phil "wrote" this one with the *New York Times'* best hockey author. This was written right after the classic Team Canada (NHL)-Russia series in September 1972. Espo's best line: "I wasn't only angry at Team Canada's critics. I was also miffed at the two guys who were invited to join us but didn't show up. There's no point in fingering them. They know who they are and the rest of us know who they are. One claimed he'd had an operation after the previous season. Bull. He didn't have any operation. And the other said he'd just put up the money for a hockey school and wanted to look after his interests. Well, hell, we'd all made sacrifices. And here Serge Savard gets cracked again while these two watch television. They'll have to live with themselves."

2. *THE BROTHERS ESPOSITO* (Associated Features). By Phil and Tony Esposito with Tim Moriarty. *Newsday* reporter Moriarty gets into the family schmaltz with the brothers. But the best line is a description of teammate Gerry Cheevers, who loves the track as much as the ice. "He loves horses, lives and breathes the sport. He claims

if there is such a thing as reincarnation, he would like to return as a horse. And he means it!"

3. *WE CAN TEACH YOU TO PLAY HOCKEY* (Associated Features). By Phil and Tony with Kevin Walsh. The best line comes from the ghost writer himself: "I'm just an old broken down goaltender who lost a couple of teeth trying to find out what this game's all about."

Longest Delay in Learning About Being Traded

On March 22, 1993, the Hartford Whalers acquired Jim Sandlak from the Vancouver Canucks. Because the clubs wanted to hide Sandlak under the cloak of "future considerations," Sandlak wasn't informed of the deal until May 17, 1993. "I played the playoffs like I was a Vancouver Canuck," says Sandlak. As a result, NHL officials pushed a new regulation, affectionately known as The Sandlak Rule — forbidding teams from hiding players under guise of "future considerations."

Boom Boom Geoffrion's Two Favorite Rocket Richard Stories

1. *Benching the Rocket.* "Maurice had the most explosive temper in the history of hockey and there were a lot of things that got him mad. He hated when the opposition played him dirty and he hated to lose but, most of all, he hated being benched. One night we were in Toronto to play the Maple Leafs and our coach Dick Irvin liked to play with

The Rocket's head. Well, he benched Maurice after the first period and you should have seen Rocket in the dressing room. You know the door by the room? Well, Dick didn't have to open it because Rocket practically walked through the closed door."

2. *Getting Rocket's Goat.* "The Rocket was one of the great scorers of all time but there were some things he never accomplished, like winning the scoring title. When he got suspended at the end of the 1954-55 season, I caught him and beat him out for the title. That was one of two scoring championships I won. I used to tell Maurice, 'There are three things in life that you never won.' Then, he would say, 'What are they?' And, I would say, 'The rookie-of-the-year and the scoring title.' So, he would say, 'What's the third one?' Then, I'd tell him, 'I'm still good-looking!' When The Rocket heard that, he would grab me and say, 'Why don't you ever say one good thing about me?' That's when I would back down."

In the category of best photo of Rocket Richard walking down The Forum corridor, this 1951 snap holds the blue ribbon. It thoroughly reveals Richard's intensity and urgency to get out on the ice and score more goals.

Gordie Howe's Two Favorite Moments

1. *Playing on the same team and same line as his sons, Mark and Marty, with the Houston Aeros.* "I had been out of hockey for a while when the World Hockey Association was organized, and when they put a team in Houston, my sons and I were given the opportunity to sign with the Aeros. For a long period of time, I had been thinking about what it would be like to play professionally with my sons and here it finally happened. I consider the moment when I lined up with them in Houston the greatest moment in my hockey life.

As Gordie Howe explains it, his biggest hockey thrill was to be able to play on a line with his sons, Mark (left) and Marty. They are lined up in pre-game warmups at Sam Houston Coliseum when they debuted with the WHA's Houston Aeros.

2. *His first National Hockey League game.* "When I look at my career from a purely individual point of view, I consider the first game that I ever played in the NHL at the top of my list. We were playing and I can vividly remember one thing: looking across the ice at the other team. All of a

sudden the idea came to me that I was going to be playing against all the guys who I had been reading about and hearing about for years. Some of them were players that I had got autographs from and now I was going to be trying to beat them. Let me tell you, that was some great moment."

Bobby Hull's Proudest Moment

"That's an easy one to answer. It was the night that I learned that my son, Brett, had signed a National Hockey League contract with the Calgary Flames. Although I knew at the time that Calgary wasn't the right team for him, I also realized that he was IN the NHL and could play on any team in the bigs. The reason I knew this is that once I played in an exhibition game with him at the University of Minnesota. I had been on the ice for only fifteen seconds alongside Brett and I could tell right then and there that the kid could play at any level. And he could be as good as he wanted to be."

Dennis Hull's Two Biggest Thrills

1. *Assisting on a landmark goal.* "My older — and more famous — brother, Bobby, was a teammate on the Chicago Blackhawks and we were playing in Boston Garden on this particular night. Bobby was shooting for his milestone 600th goal and at one point in the game I wound up on the ice with him. Usually, I liked to crank up the big slapshot but this time I heard Bobby yell, 'GIMME THE PUCK!' I had no choice but to give it to him, so I did and he went in and scored. Let me tell you, that was not one of my cheap assists."

2. *Sitting next to Gordie Howe in an All-Star Game.* "I was a 22-year-old kid when I played in my first National Hockey League All-Star Gme. We were at The Forum in Montreal and on the afternoon of the game, I told the All-Stars' trainer that I'd like to sit next to Gordie Howe. I couldn't believe it but then he told me, 'Gordie called me today and said that he wanted to sit next to you.' Sure enough, he did and it was the thrill of my life. Except, after the game, I heard that Gordie told a reporter, 'I'm never going to sit next to Dennis Hull again because he talks too much!'"

Dennis Hull's Favorite Putdown of Himself

"In the Hull family, there's Bobby and Brett who became NHL stars, so I didn't have a chance to be the best in my family. And if my sister had been able to play, I would have been fourth-best in the family!"

Dennis Hull's Two Favorite Putdowns of San Jose Sharks Rookie Pat Falloon When Hull Was a TV Analyst

1. *The Kid is too fat.* "I said that the number one draft pick looked like The Pillsbury Doughboy and I changed his name to 'Fatty Balloon.'"

2. *The Kid wouldn't backcheck.* "Pat wasn't very good defensively so one night I said, 'The only way to get Falloon back in his own end is to play the national anthem.'

Dennis Hull's Two Other Favorite Quips While Broadcasting in the San Francisco Bay Area

1. *Putting down a referee.* "Rob Schick was handling this particular game and there happened to be a loose stick on the ice which he didn't see. Next thing you know, the ref fell right over it. When I saw that I said, 'This is the first time I had seen Schick on a stick!'"

2. *Spoofing the Bay Area's Gay Community.* "When I was broadcasting in San Francisco, I couldn't say a lot of things that I could when I was working games in other cities. For example, I was never allowed to use the expression, 'Back-to-back home games.' And I couldn't say, 'Now we'll see the men separated from the boys.'"

Jacques Demers' Most Inspirational Eight Words

Before Game Five of the 1993 Stanley Cup finals, Demers addressed his players in the dressing room before the opening face-off. He declared, "Remember who you are. Remember what you represent." After hearing that, the Montreal Canadiens scored in the opening minute and went on to win the Stanley Cup.

Strangest Reason To Fire a Good Coach

Tom Webster was one of the most respected coaches in the Ontario Hockey League in 1993, leading the Detroit Junior

Red Wings. But Webster lost out to family ties. It happened this way: Tommy's teenage daughter was dating a player on the Junior Wings and, for this reason, he was fired. Apparently Webster had violated a policy of Compuware Corporation, owner of the team. Webster was given an ultimatum: bring an end to the relationship or face dismissal. When he took no action, he was fired. "Tommy was caught between company policy and a family situation," said Junior Wings general manager Jim Rutherford. "I gave Tommy time to think it through before the termination took place. Nothing changed. I did what I had to do. I had no choice." Webster soon found himself a job as assistant coach of the Florida Panthers who have no rules about coaches' daughters dating players on the team.

Four Women Who Broke the All-Male Public Relations Barrier in the NHL

1. *Susie Mathieu.* She was the pioneer. Mathieu's career began in 1975 as an assistant in the St. Louis Blues' publicity department when the franchise was owned by Sid Salomon, Jr. and his son, Sid III. In 1977, she was named public relations director and is now vice president, director of marketing and public relations.

2. *Cindy Himes.* One of the most difficult assignments has been handling publicity for a team that has had Mario Lemieux as its superstar. Himes has done that through the Pittsburgh Penguins Stanley Cup-winning years, 1992 and 1993, continuing at the post to this day.

3. *Heidi Holland.* She did her basic training with the Hartford Whalers and then hedgehopped across New

England to take over the P.R. directorship of the Bruins. It wasn't easy following the large footsteps of legendary Nate Greenberg.

4. *Ginger Killian.* A whiz-bang in the Fordham University athletic department, the strikingly attractive publicist originally was hired by the New York Rangers as a P.R. aide and moved to the top job with the New York Islanders in 1992. Her husband, Steve Serby, is football columnist for the *New York Post.*

GLENN ANDERSON'S TWO FLAKIEST MOMENTS

1. *The Sleeping Alibi.* As a member of the Edmonton Oilers, the fleet forward missed an 11 o'clock practice even though he had been awakened four hours earlier. Teammate Kevin Lowe said he couldn't believe Anderson's explanation to coach Glen Sather: "Slats, I was up real early and I was cruising around my apartment having a good time. And I dozed off!" According to Lowe, Sather nearly got a case of lockjaw after hearing the alibi.

2. *The Broadcast Squelch.* During an interview with Minnesota broadcaster Rob Leer, Anderson was asked on the air what it would mean to him if the North Stars beat Toronto for the final playoff berth. Glenn blithely replied, "Sex on the beach!" And said no more.

The best conga-line hockey fight photo. The principals are goalie Doug Favell (far right) of the Philadelphia Flyers and Reg Fleming (third from right) of the New York Rangers. Separating them is Lou Angotti. The fascinated referee looking on at the far left is John Ashley. The flying glove belongs to Fleming, who believed it looked better on Favell's head.

JAROMIR JAGR'S TWO FAVORITE DEPARTMENT STORE CAPERS

1. *Pretending to be a poor refugee.* On a shopping trip with Penguins teammate Martin Straka, the Czech-born Jagr walked to the suitcase section of a Pittsburgh department store. The saleswoman, who didn't recognize them, produced a valise that cost $200. Jagr feigned shock. "Oh, no, oh, no," he said while nudging Straka. "We are poor, poor, immigrants from Czechoslovakia. We no have that kind of money." Jagr persisted with the story until the guilt-ridden saleswoman halved the price.

2. *Pretending to be a woman to avoid adoring fans.* Jagr was trapped in a department store by a horde of fans. Jaromir conducted an orderly retreat to the women's department purchased a long, blond wig, put his arm around Straka and passed him off as Martin's adoring girlfriend for the rest of their shopping and escaped through the line of fans.

JACQUES DEMERS' TWO MOST EMBARRASSING MOMENTS AS A COACH

1. *The Unbreakable Instruction Stick.* One night, while coaching the Detroit Red Wings, Demers got into a snit. To hammer home a point, Jacques tried to break the wooden instruction stick on the blackboard. But every time he banged, the stick richocheted off the board with no damage. Demers banged with greater and greater ferocity, like a tympanist developing a crescendo. "The darn thing wouldn't break," recalls Shawn Burr, who played for Jacques at the time. "So right then and there Glen Hanlon reached over and handed him his goalie stick. That broke up the meeting."

2. *The Glen Hanlon Stopper.* During the 1987 playoffs, Demers' Red Wings were down three games to one to Toronto when Jacques summoned his players to a hotel room meeting. The coach went from player to player, asking each one what had to be done to win. Everybody had a serious answer until he got to Glen Hanlon. When Jacques asked him what was on his mind, the goalie said, "Coach, I was just sitting here thinking how they get those lights to go up and down on that big sign on the building across the street." Every player nearly fell over backwards in his chair, laughing. "Then," Hanlon recalls, "we went out and won three straight — and the series!"

Referee Paul Stewart's Best On-Ice Putdowns

1. *Against Al Iafrate.* While attempting to ice the puck, the defenseman fired the rubber off Stewart's derriere. A few minutes later, Iafrate rang the puck along the boards, missing Stewart by a hair. "Paul skated over to me," Iafrate remembers, "and said he was going to kick my ass. And he repeated it throughout the game."

2. *Against Guy Lafleur.* Before retirement, The Flower took to wearing an elaborate toupee and the referee immediately took note of it. When the Hall of Famer lined up for a face-off, Stewart dead-panned, "What are you using, Guy, Rapid Grow?" Then, a pause, "Hey, I'd better go get some." Stewart adds, "Guy laughed but then told me to drop the puck, which was his way of telling me to shut up."

3. *Against a French Canadian.* Although Stewart is bilingual, few French-Canadian players are aware that he speaks French. "There was a game," Stewart says, "when one of them was calling me every name in the book — in French, of course. I skated over and asked — in French — if he had the money to pay for the penalty I was about to give him."

Three Cherished Assets of Chicago Stadium To Be Mourned in Its Passing

1. *The Organ.* The Stadium's organ was the biggest of any arena's on the continent and was well-played by a host of organists from Al Melgard to Nancy Faust. The only equivalent organ sound is produced in Radio City Music Hall.

2. *The Star Spangled Banner Roar.* Blackhawks fans would begin an electrifying cheer the moment vocalist Wayne Messmer began the first chorus of the national anthem. Then they would build to a wild, frenzied finish that often left opposition players in a state of shock.

3. *The Second Balcony Overhang.* Unlike contemporary arenas, the Stadium boasted not one, but two balconies. The second (upper) balcony overhung the ice, giving those in the first three rows a distinct feeling of being right on top of the play. Which, in fact, they were.

NAME THE ONLY RETIRED PROFESSIONAL SOCCER PLAYER, PROFESSIONAL MUSICIAN AND LINGUIST WHO IS A PREMIER NHL ICE-MAKER

Roberto Borzomi of Long Island speaks four languages, played pro soccer in Italy, and still makes a buck on music. But the smiling Italian-American's claim to fame is the quality of ice he makes at Nassau Coliseum for the New York Islanders home games. "When Roberto makes the ice," says Irene Virag of *Newsday*, "he is an artist. A grand master on a grand scale whose canvas is the 200-foot by 85-foot rink. It is there that he is in his element as he mixes bright blues and deep reds, as he wields buckets and brushes and measuring tapes and uses a fine eye for detail and a 180-foot long firehose to create his masterpiece."

Gump Worsley's Two Best Wisecracks

1. *Deploring his defense.* When Worsley played goal for the New York Rangers, the Broadway Blueshirts hardly were *la crème de la crème* of the NHL. After a particularly tough loss, Worsley was interviewed by a magazine writer. "Which team in the league gives you the most trouble?" the interviewer wondered. Without missing a beat, The Gumper shot back, "THE RANGERS!" And he meant it, too.

2. *Deploring his coach.* The Gump's coach for a couple of years was volatile Phil Watson, a notorious sore loser and blame-thrower. On this night his Rangers had lost a heartbreaker and Watson was asked about the defeat in the post-game post mortem with the media. A reporter asked Watson what the problem was and the coach snapped, "How can we win when we have a goalie [Worsley] with a beer-barrel belly?"

   After hearing that, the journalists marched directly to Worsley's locker room stall and asked for his rebuttal. To which, The Gump barked, "It just shows you how little he knows — I NEVER DRINK ANYTHING BUT JOHNNY WALKER RED!"

Three Reasons Why Gordie Howe Will Always Rank Above Wayne Gretzky on the All-Time List of Great Scorers

1. *Point Value.* When Howe played most of his NHL hockey, the majors consisted of a six-team league in which scoring was held to a minimum. Howe's 49 goals in one season would be the equivalent of 98 goals in the present free-scoring era.

2. *Longevity.* Nobody has played at a higher level for a longer time than Howe. Gordie broke into the NHL immediately after World War II and still was playing after the NHL merger with the WHA. Thus, he surpassed four decades of major league play. After 15 years in the NHL, Gretzky is talking about retirement.

3. *Dimensions.* Gordie was the ultimate multi-dimensional player. He could play defense — and actually did for one season as a Detroit Red Wing — was the hardest-hitting forward in history, backchecked with the best and, of course, was an offensive marvel. While Wayne has been the most productive player of all time, his game essentially has been limited to offense. He always has been too fragile to bodycheck and is wanting defensively.

Two Significant Women Who Have Been Involved in Men's Hockey

1. *Laura Stamm.* Originator of the "Power Skating" technique, Stamm has worked with more NHL players on improving their strides than any other instructor, male or female. Stamm's first NHL pupil was New York Islanders right wing Bob Nystrom who, two years after enrolling with Laura, scored the Isles' Stanley Cup-winning overtime goal in 1980. Among her other students are goalie Kelly Hrudey and penalty-killer Doug Brown.

2. *Manon Rheaume.* After breaking through the all-male playing barrier in Quebec Junior hockey, Rheaume then did it on the professional level after the Tampa Bay Lightning signed her to a contract. The attractive puck-stopper worked out with the NHL club but eventually wound up playing against men in the East Coast Hockey

League and in the summer of 1994 in Roller Hockey International.

Ten Most Appropriate Names

1. *Mario Lemieux.* What could be more fitting? One of hockey's all-time greats has a name that translates as "The Better."

2. *Larry Playfair.* The man had 1,812 career penalty minutes yet played the game hard and, occasionally, clean.

3. *Lindy Ruff.* Now this is more like it. This hard-hitter has 1,264 career penalty minutes and, yes, he was rough.

4. *Joseph Ironstone.* Appropriately, he was a goaltender.

5. *Hubert Quackenbush.* Otherwise known as Bill, this distinguished player carried a distinguished name. He was one of the cleanest, most proficient defensemen of all time.

6. *Ebeneezer Goodfellow.* Alias Ebbie. He is the only Ebeneezer of renown — or even non-renown — in the NHL. And, yes, he was a good fellow. Furthermore, he was one of the best players in the pre-World War II NHL with the Detroit Red Wings.

7. *Frank McCool.* While he wasn't as cool as Georges Vezina, The Chicoutimi Cucumber, McCool was cool enough to register three consecutive shutouts in the first three games of the 1945 Stanley Cup finals.

8. *Maxwell Herbert Lloyd (Max) Bentley*. A sweetheart of a name for a sweetheart of a hockey player; arguably the best stickhandler ever.

9. *Christian Ruuttu*. If you think it's tough spelling his last name, try his hometown — Lappeenranta, Finland.

10. *Eric Vail*. He never played for the Colorado Rockies, but he sure would have been a hit in ski country, wouldn't he?

Bill "Wee Willie" Mosienko, who died in the summer of 1994, holds a record that never will be broken. On March 23, 1952 he scored three goals in 21 seconds against the New York Rangers at Madison Square Garden. Mosienko, who played his entire career with the Chicago Blackhawks, once was a member of the famed Pony Line with Max and Doug Bentley.

Ten Unusual Birthplaces

1. *Forks of Credit, Ontario.* This hamlet, which once was on the map, no longer exists. But it has the distinction of being the home to one former NHL player, Aldo Guidolin, who played for the Rangers in the mid-to-late 1950s.

2. *Flin Flon, Manitoba.* Named after a fictional character called Josiah Flintabatty Flonerton, Flin Flon is the birthplace of no less than 13 NHL and WHA players including Bobby Clarke, Dean Evason, and long-retired NHL veteran Eric Nesterenko.

3. *South Porcupine, Ontario.* Bear in mind there is no North, West or East Porcupine. But from the South came seven NHL players, including 1962 Toronto Maple Leafs Stanley Cup ace Bob Nevin.

4. *Porcupine Plain, Saskatchewan.* Speaking of the spiny backed critters, this Porcupine is home to Kelly Chase, who sometimes is as irksome as a porcupine's quills.

5. *Shuswap, British Columbia.* If you think that's a funny name, remember it's the birthplace of Ollie Reinika, who played on the original (1926-27) New York Rangers. For a short time, the Blueshirts' publicists actually had his name changed to Ollie Rocco so that fans would think he was of Italian rather than Finnish descent and therefore would descend on Madison Square Garden to see him play. They didn't!

6. *Potlatch, Idaho.* The most amazing thing is that not one but two pro hockey players came from this unlikely outpost. One was Guyle Fielder, the most productive minor leaguer of all time. The other was Pat Shea.

7. *Staten Island, New York.* Stuck in the middle of New York Bay is an island borough of New York City that somehow managed to produce one NHL player, Nick Fotiu, ex of the Rangers.

8. *Come by Chance, Newfoundland.* Come by luck, Newfy product Robert Gladney had a cup of coffee with the Kings and Penguins between 1982 and 1984.

9. *Rocky Mountain House, Alberta.* This House is home to Dean Magee who played for the North Stars in the NHL and Indianapolis of the WHA.

10. *100-Mile House, British Columbia.* Doug Robinson, once the brightest of NHL prospects, but turned out to be a dull disappoinment, is the 100-Mile House contribution to the bigs.

Seven Countries You'd Never Expect to Produce NHL Players

1. *Formosa.* Rod Langway, the best defenseman in the history of the Washington Capitals, launched his life in the Orient.

2. *South Korea.* A defenseman on Pittsburgh's two Stanley Cup-winners, Jim Paek still returns to his native land during the off-season.

3. *South Africa.* There are plenty of gold mines, but not many rinks and only one NHL goalie product, Olaf Kolzig.

4. *Paraguay.* How Willi Plett got from Asunción to Atlanta only he can explain.

5. *Jamaica.* One of the few black players to have made it to the NHL, Graeme Townshend got to the top — albeit briefly — from the West Indies, via Canada.

6. *Haiti.* Another black player who briefly starred with the New Jersey Devils, Claude Vilgrain learned his hockey in the province of Quebec after his family moved north.

7. *Brazil.* Not exactly a household name, Mike Greenlay appropriately went from Rio to a cup of coffee in the NHL.

The Three Most Misspelled Names

1. *Terry Sawchuk.* The mistakes weren't made by Canadians but rather American editors and writers unfamiliar with the Ukrainian spelling. Invariably, it came out Terry Sawchuck, which may have looked right but was very wrong. Others like Sawchuk who lost out to the illiterate editors are Clint Malarchuk, Dave Andredychuk, Dale Hawerchuk, Dennis Sobchuk, and oodles of other Chuks, including the ever-popular Igor Kravchuk.

2. *Jim Thomson.* The star defenseman on Toronto Maple Leafs Stanley Cup-winners in 1947, 1948, 1949 and 1951, Thomson enjoyed his heyday during the same era as New York Giants baseball ace Bobby Thomson. Both were victimized by reporters who insisted on spelling it Thompson. Ech!

3. *Stephen Wojciechowski.* The erstwhile Detroit right wing caused so much trouble for the writing fraternity, the Red Wings publicity asked newsmen simply to refer to him as "Steve Wochy." They were delighted to oblige.

Although Mike Keenan received considerable publicity for walking out on his coaching job following the 1994 playoffs, he wasn't the first Rangers coach to do so. Lynn Patrick — son of Hall-of-Famer Lester Patrick and father of Penguins GM Craig Patrick — took the Rangers to the seventh game of the 1950 Cup finals. Although New York was eliminated in the second sudden-death overtime, Patrick was hailed as a hero on Broadway.

THE TOP TEN BY NATIONS

FINLAND

1. *Jari Kurri*. After Mike Bossy, Wayne Gretzky's sidekick ranks as the best right wing of the past 15 years.

2. *Esa Tikkanen*. An underrated member of the Edmonton Oilers Stanley Cup-winners. And a very good reason why the New York Rangers broke their 54-year Cup drought in 1994.

3. *Teemu Selanne*. If his NHL rookie season is a barometer, the jolly Jet eventually could be the best Finn ever.

Unfortunately, an injury-plagued sophomore year put the brakes on Teemu.

4. *Tomas Sandstrom.* Mistakenly labelled a Swede, Tomas not only is Finn-born, but the dirtiest Finland native ever to reach the NHL, Esa Tikkanen included.

5. *Jyrki Lumme.* By far the most underrated Finn, Lumme is a defenseman who has played remarkably well at every NHL stop, most recently Vancouver where he helped the Canucks to the 1994 Stanley Cup finals.

6. *Reijo Ruotsalainen.* Pound for pound the most gifted Finn, Double R starred for the New York Rangers in the mid-1980s and might have become a First All-Star had he owned ten more pounds on his fuselage.

7. *Jari Gronstrand.* Like Lumme, Gronstrand has played commendably but without the flash of a Ruotsalainen and, as a result, his gifts have been muted.

8. *Mikko Makela.* During his first NHL go-round as a New York Islander, the blond beauty was too immature to be totally effective. He might be better the second time around. He's one of the most lyrical skaters and packs a nifty shot.

9. *Illka Sinisalo.* He provided Philadelphia Flyers fans with many a thrill.

10. *Christian Ruuttu.* Based on his native talent and his build-up as a Buffalo Sabre, Christian should have turned into a better player than he has, and will finish his career with people wondering what might have been.

SWEDEN

1. *Bob Nystrom.* No other Swede could claim that he scored a Stanley Cup-winning goal in sudden-death overtime as Nystrom did for the New York Islanders in 1980.

2. *Mats Naslund.* During the years he spent with the Montreal Canadiens, the little speed merchant was one of the most effective point-producers this side of Stockholm.

3. *Ulf Nilsson.* One can only wonder how high Nilsson's star would have climbed had he not been curtailed by serious injury. He was one of the best products of the WHA.

4. *Anders Hedberg.* On a WHA line with Nilsson and Bobby Hull, Hedberg gives new meaning to class. Anders was at his best in the 1979 playoffs, upsetting the New York Islanders in six games.

5. *Ulf Samuelsson.* The most vicious Swede to emerge on the NHL scene, Ulfie was a prime reason why the Pittsburgh Penguins won the Stanley Cup in 1991 and 1992.

6. *Kjell Samuelsson.* Otherwise known as The Human Tripod, this long fellow was remarkably adroit and tough. His size enabled him to become one of the NHL's finest pokecheckers.

7. *Thomas Steen.* Winnipeg critics will tell you that year in and year out, the Jets never obtained a more consistent performer. They are right.

8. *Niklas Lidstrom.* While it still is relatively early in his career, Lidstrom is displaying enough talent to suggest a possible All-Star berth in the future.

9. *Calle Johansson*. The Washington Capitals have been a better team because of his steady but unobtrusive work behind the blue line.

10. *Mikael Andersson*. A player in the Mikko Makela mold, Andersson promised more than he delivered. Still, there have been many a nifty play on his stick.

Czechoslovakia

1. *Stan Mikita*. Along with Jean Beliveau and Wayne Gretzky, Stosh ranks among the top centers of all time. His only debit — he played on only one Stanley Cup-winner (Chicago Blackhawks, 1961).

2. *Peter Stastny*. Best of the three Slovak-born brothers (Marian and Anton are the others), Peter is a sure-thing to gain entrance to The Hockey Hall of Fame. He helped put the Quebec Nordiques on the map.

3. *Jaromir Jagr*. No less an authority than Mario Lemieux opines that Jagr could be the best player in the NHL if he puts his mind to it. Jagr starred for the Pittsburgh Penguins 1991 and 1992 Stanley Cup-winners.

4. *Frank Musil*. The crafty defenseman's problem was that he didn't have a good press agent. Skating in Minnesota and Calgary, he's been egregiously overlooked despite excellent play year in and year out.

5. *Petr Nedved*. The raw talent is huge but maturity still is necessary to harness the goods. He could be the most gifted Czech to hit North America since Stan Mikita.

6. *Robert Reichel.* Very quietly, Reichel has won kudos among his peers for a multi-dimensional game appreciated more by coaches than fans.

7. *Bobby Holik.* There are few stronger players with harder shots than Holik. His problem has been an inability to put all facets of his game in one surging package. If he ever does, look out!

8. *Anton Stastny.* Although he departed the NHL long before Peter, this Stastny was an effective contributor, especially when working on a line with his older brother.

9. *Vladimir Ruzicka.* Some of his moves were enough to have enemy coaches drooling in envy. Unfortunately, Vlad was terribly inconsistent and had no idea where to find the defensive zone.

10. *Marian Stastny.* Eldest of the three brothers, Marian at one time was the best, but that was in Europe. By the time he reached the NHL, his major skills had been eroded. Still, he was a winner.

RUSSIA

1. *Sergei Fedorov.* All one need examine is the 1994 NHL awards list to appreciate the comprehensive talents of the Detroit sharpshooter. How many players can boast a Hart Trophy and Selke Trophy in one season?

2. *Pavel Bure.* The Vancouver Canucks opened the bank for The Russian Rocket and while nobody is really worth his millions, Bure certainly has become one of the marquee players of the 1990s.

3. *Alexander Mogilny.* Guts, goals and glamor are the trademarks of Buffalo's superstar who even had the distinction of being named captain in the absence of teammate Pat LaFontaine in 1993-94.

4. *Slava Fetisov.* The Bobby Orr of the Soviet Union, Fetisov arrived in New Jersey too late to display that talents that made him Mister Hockey in Russia. Still, he has played competently and nobly for the Devils.

5. *Sergei Makarov.* Despite problems with then-Calgary coach Terry Crisp, Sergei performed brilliantly in spurts for Calgary and picked up where he left off after being dealt to San Jose.

6. *Igor Larionov.* One of the niftiest stickhandlers to emigrate from Europe, Igor teamed expertly with old pal Makarov to steam the Sharks to a playoff berth in 1993-93 and then a surprisingly stirring playoff run.

7. *Alexei Kovalev.* Historians are suggesting — with considerably evidence — that the dipsy-doodling center-right wing is a latter-day Max Bentley, which is praise from Attica.

8. *Sergei Nemchinov.* Easily the best overlooked New York Ranger during the 1992-94 period, Nemchinov can score, can check and can kill penalties.

9. *Dmitri Khristich.* The Washington Capitals were frustrated by DK's failure to exploit all his offensive talents but they also understand that they'd never have been a playoff contender without his contributions.

10. *Vladimir Malakhov*. The New York Islanders believe that Vlad has Norris Trophy potential but they're not sure how to extract it from this big, long-striding defenseman. If he ever screws his head on straight, he'll be among the best.

U.S.A.

1. *Joe Mullen*. This product of New York City's sidewalks has done more offensive work for more years than any of his compatriots. What's more, he also has two Stanley Cup rings (1971, 1972) from the Pittsburgh Penguins.

2. *Pat Lafontaine*. Kid Lightning of the New York Islanders has become Leader Lightning with the Buffalo Sabres. He's a crafty offensive machine who was unfortunately stalled in 1993-94 by a serious knee injury.

3. *Brian Leetch*. The Connecticut product has a repertoire of offensive weaponry that is absolutely dazzling. Though a bit soft in his own end, Leetch is improving in that department as well.

4. *Mike Modano*. All that was needed to round out the Detroiter's game was a touch of leadership, and now that appears to be falling into place. In two years, he could be a Hart Trophy-winner.

5. *Ken Morrow*. The New York Islanders dynastic run of four consecutive Stanley Cups never would have been possible without Ken's quiet but effective defense and extremely timely sudden-death playoff goals.

6. *Neal Broten*. From the Minnesota rinks to the North Stars and, more recently, the Dallas Stars, capsulizes a very pro-

ductive career. The smallish forward is like Joe Mullen in many positive ways.

7. *John Vanbiesbrouck.* Uncle Sam has produced many a top goaltender, but Beezer has been the best American puck-stopper of the past decade.

8. *Kevin Hatcher.* The Washington Capitals didn't name him captain for nothing. Another Detroit product who has come through, Kevin is immense in many ways but mostly as a solid defenseman.

9. *Chris Chelios.* A graduate of the 1984 U.S. Olympic Team, Chelly is the most intense American defender to come down the pike. He is totally fearless and, perhaps, too often reckless. But he is a champ.

10. *Brian Mullen.* Overshadowed by his older brother, Brian nonetheless has withstood the test of time with the New York Rangers, Winnipeg Jets and New York Islanders. He's arguably the best American-born utility player to grace the NHL.

The Three Best — and Last — Players To Wear Regular Glasses in the NHL

1. *Al Arbour.* Alger's career spanned 1953-54 through 1970-71 and included stops in Detroit, Chicago, Toronto and St. Louis. Never an All-Star, the bespectacled one was an honest workman and one of the best defensive defensemen.

2. *Hal Laycoe.* From 1945-46 through 1955-56, Laycoe played a stalwart defensive game starting with the Rangers, then the Montreal Canadiens and, finally, the Boston Bruins, always with a pair of specs over his eyes.

3. *Clint Albright.* It remains a mystery why the Rangers only kept Albright for only the 1948-49 season. He was a forward with many assets but, obviously, they eluded the eyesight of management. Maybe the front office needed the same kind of eyeglasses worn by Clint.

THE FIVE BEST MAYHEM-INSPIRING NAMES

1. Garth Butcher.

2. Adam Graves.

3. Darren Rumble.

4. Bob Corkum.

5. Stu Grimson.

FOUR REASONS WHY THE WINNIPEG JETS WERE DRAFT DISASTERS

1. *Jimmy Mann.* The 1979 draft was considered one of the best ever. The Jets could have selected either Kevin Lowe or Michel Goulet with their 19th pick. Instead, they opted for Jimmy Mann who scored 10 goals and 20 assists in eight NHL seasons.

2. *Andrew McBain.* What a wonderful year 1983 was, as the New York Islanders nabbed Pat LaFontaine in the draft while the Detroit Red Wings opted for Steve Yzerman. Yikes! The Jets had two picks and with them, they chose, McBain and...

3. *Bobby Dollas.*

4. *Nobody.* Alas, in 1984, when Mario Lemieux, Kirk Muller and Gary Roberts were nabbed, Winnipeg dealt their first pick to Pittsburgh as part of compensation for Randy Carlyle. That pick was used by the Penguins to obtain Doug Bodger, who surfaced as one of the most dependable defensemen of the last ten years.

THE FIRST PLAYER EVER DRAFTED TWICE

Joe Reekie — In 1983, the gabby defenseman was picked by the Hartford Whalers in the seventh round. However, the Whalers failed to sign The Reekster, so he returned to Junior hockey and prepared to go to college. However, the Buffalo Sabres intervened and drafted Joe in the sixth round of the 1985 draft. To which Smilin' Joe opines, "Wait until I'm 30, I'll be a first-rounder. Other guys have been drafted twice, but I was first. I'm getting in that record book one way or another — I'm part of history." In more ways than one — Reekie holds the unofficial NHL record for more dressing room gab than any defenseman between 1989 and 1994.

The Worst Case of Foot-in-Draft Disease, as Recorded by Terry Crisp

Tampa Bay Lightning coach Terry Crisp attended the 1981 draft when Barry Tobobondung was a candidate for selection. Tobobondung's father, Les, was chief of the Indian reservation on Parry Island, near Crisp's hometown, Parry Sound, Ontario.

Crisp watched with special interest when Barry's name was called out by the Philadelphia Flyers. "He was way the hell up in the rafters at the Montreal Forum," Crisp remembers, "but he's coming down to the floor. He's so excited, he doesn't even bother using steps; he's climbing over seats. Well, his foot falls right through one of those old wooden seats, between the part that folds up and the seat back. Can't get out. He was up there for two hours. They had to take the whole row apart with wrenches. Funniest thing you ever saw. But the kid was still waving. He was so happy." That's the good news. The bad news is that Barry Tobobondung never played a game in the National Hockey League.

The Ten Best Hockey Stories of the '30s and '40s, as Told By Hall-of-Fame Goalie Chuck Rayner

1. *The Case of the Oversized Pads.*
   "I broke into the NHL with the New York Americans, which was the other big-league hockey club in New York before World War II along with the Rangers. Our manager and coach was a very colorful fellow named Red Dutton, who had been a fiery defenseman with the Amerks before he took over the team. On this night we were in Chicago,

playing the Blackhawks, who were coached by an equally fiery fellow named Paul Thompson. In those days (1941-42), the rules and regulations on goalie pad size were pretty tough. They had to be just the right size, otherwise there was a penalty. But the thing was that as each goalie breaks in his pads, they automatically get wider because of all the moisture and stuff. Well, in the middle of the game, Thompson calls over the referee and says, 'There's something wrong with those pads of Rayner's. You'd better measure them.' And, sure enough, they were too wide. But Dutton was no dope. He realizes what's going on and he calls the referee to him, pointing to the Chicago goalie, Mike Karakas. 'All right,' says Red, 'go and measure Karakas.' So they got out the tape again and measured Mike. What do you know! His were too wide, as well, so they cancelled both penalties, and we finished the game with oversized pads on both sides. As soon as we got back to New York, I had a new set of pads."

The distinction of being the only NHL team ever owned by a bootlegger belonged to the New York Americans, who were coached by Red Dutton (left) and backed by William "Big Bill" Dwyer, whose son William A. Dwyer, helps Dutton sign a contract — as if Red needed any help.

2. *The Toughness of Eddie Shore.*
    "Before I reached the NHL, I played my minor league hockey with the Americans farm team in Springfield, Massachusetts. Shore was something else; he not only owned the Indians, he did everything at that Eastern States Coliseum rink, including coaching and managing the team. Eddie even managed to play one season with the Amerks while *also* playing for his Springfield club. Eddie had been one of the greatest defensemen in NHL history and was a very, very demanding man. His wife, a wonderful lady named Kate McRae, once told me, 'Eddie's a kook.' When you played for Shore, you had to expect the totally unorthodox. He would have his players learn tap-dancing for agility, and do all sorts of seemingly weird things, including exercises for goaltenders. I still say that Shore was the greatest goaltending coach I ever had in my life. He stressed angle goaltending and following up your defensemen. Plus, he was very strong on balance. You had to skate to please him. After practice, he would fill a couple of pails with pucks and tell me, 'Take one hand and just keep clearing that puck from the net.' It got so that my hand was so sore that I couldn't move it. I'd tell him, 'Eddie, I can't do it anymore.' When he heard that, he'd come right back and tell me, 'Well, stay out another hour.' The less you said to Shore the better, because he could be real different. He wouldn't ask you to do anything that he wasn't willing to do himself, and I always admired him for that."

3. *A Strange Route to the NHL.*
    Naturally, my goal was to make it to the NHL, but I was willing to bide my time and pay my dues in Springfield. One night the Indians were playing Pittsburgh, which then was a farm team of the Toronto Maple Leafs. The

score was 1-1 when one of their defensemen let a shot go from outside the blue line. The puck hit me high and bounced down in front of me. Shore was playing defense for us and yelled at me, 'I got it!' All of a sudden — whoosh! — the puck is in the net and we're down 2-1 to a team we really wanted to beat. Shore was on with another defenseman named Frank Beisler. We ended up losing, 2-1, and afterwards in the dressing room, Shore came and me and roared, 'IT'S YOUR FAULT WE LOST.' I said, 'Eddie, what do you mean it's my fault? For heaven's sake, I made the save in the first place. YOU SCORED THE GOAL FOR THEM. You were trying to clear it and it went into the net.' He ordered me out of the dressing room but I wouldn't leave, so he said to me, 'You've got to go out and practice for another half-hour to an hour.' I snapped, 'I'm not going. That's it! I can't take this anymore. Eddie, you've been on my neck since I got here.' Just then, two of the veterans, Beisler and Max Kaminsky, chirped in, 'Leave the kid alone; you're gonna ruin him.' With that, Shore announces to me, 'You've got a hundred dollar fine.' Let me tell you, at that time $100 was a lot of money and I was steamed. I walked over to Shore and barked, 'There's your pads; everything that you own. Good luck. I'm not gonna play for you anymore. I'm calling Dutton.' And I did. Next thing you know, Dutton phoned Shore and told him, 'Get that kid on the next plane to New York and do it quick. And that fine you gave him is not going to stand.' That was the end of it — I took the plane to New York and found out the most unbelievable thing. The Americans goalie, Earl Robertson, was playing against Detroit that night and broke his collarbone. So, it turned out that I would have been called up anyway."

4. *Red Dutton vs. Lester Patrick.*
"In addition to being a terrific defenseman and a wonderful coach, Dutton was a marvelous character. He was full of energy and emotion and was very devoted to the Americans. Red knew that the Amerks had preceded the Rangers into Madison Square Garden, but that the Garden people owned the Rangers and we had to pay rent. That meant that the Rangers always got a better deal from the Garden and we got the short end of the stick. Another thing was that the Rangers, who were run by Lester Patrick, had won three Stanley Cups with the Rangers, and Red had none with the Amerks. It's a shame that a great guy like Dutton never won a Cup because he would still be celebrating. So, you can imagine that Red and Lester never got along and always were going at each other, not to mention the two teams. One incident tells a lot about the two of them. We were playing the Rangers at the Garden, and the benches were side by side. Whenever there was a dispute between the clubs — which was often — Patrick would hold up his hand and flash his Stanley Cup ring and say, 'Red, did you ever see one of these?' Red, who had a temper that matched his hair, would just go straight up, throwing one of his white hats and kicking sticks."

5. *When the Brooklyn Americans weren't.*
"New York got its first NHL team in 1925 when a bootlegger named Big Bill Dwyer bought the Hamilton franchise and moved it to Manhattan. The Amerks played out of Madison Square Garden from the very beginning and were called the New York Americans, which is the way it should have been. But in 1941-42, when I was with the team, the team name was changed to Brooklyn Americans and there's a funny story behind it. At the

time, all the single fellows on the Amerks lived in the Piccadilly Hotel, a block from Times Square, and a few blocks south of the Garden. At this particular point in the season, we were in a terrific slump and Dutton was getting hotter and hotter. Finally, he says, 'I know what's wrong. You guys are spending too much time on Broadway. I'm gonna move the whole bunch of you outta there and move you to Brooklyn. And we're gonna change the name of the team to the Brooklyn Americans." So, Dutton booked us into a Brooklyn hotel which was a real dump. Art Chapman, who was coaching us at the time, looked at the hotel and said, 'We're not staying here.' So, we got back on the bus and went right back to the Piccadilly without saying a thing to Dutton. Nobody said a word and none of the newspapermen knew about it, either. We were in the Piccadilly again and everything was fine. Geez, then we win a couple of games and we're on a hot streak. Well, I'll tell you, Dutton's chest was all puffed up. He says, 'I knew it all along. You guys were playing too much on Broadway Now that I've got you over in Brooklyn, we're winning.' Nobody tells Red that we're back at the Piccadilly until we take off on a road trip. We're sitting with Red in the corner of the Pullman train and Dutton finds out we're back on Broadway. What does he do? He breaks up laughing and says, 'What a crazy bugger I am.' But the P.S. to the story is this: we kept 'Brooklyn' on our jerseys for the rest of the season although we played all our home games in Madison Square Garden."

6. *The Game that Almost Wasn't.*
"When I broke into the NHL, almost all the travel was done by train. We'd often play a game on Saturday night in Toronto and then board the train for the trip to New

York for a Sunday night game at home. Every year or so, the trains would get caught in a big blizzard and we'd get into the rink just before game time. Once we had a game with the Red Wings at the Garden and both clubs got hung up on the train in western New York. We didn't get to the rink until 10:30 at night, which was two hours after game time. What they did was suit up a bunch of amateur players who were in the stands, and they entertained the fans until we got there. That night I shut out Detroit 1-0. But the snow story that I'm most fond of took place in Chicago. This time we were heading west on the train and ran right into a terrific blizzard in Upstate New York. By the time we got to Buffalo, the train couldn't move anymore so we got off the Pullman and took a bus to Cleveland. From there we took another train to Chicago and as soon as we reached the station, a police escort rushed us to Chicago Stadium. By this time it was almost eleven at night, but there were more than 16,000 people filling the arena. Alex Kaleta, who had been an old pal of mine but was playing for the Blackhawks at the time, came onto the ice to take a face-off. He skated over to my crease, looked up at the screaming fans and said to me, 'Charlie, isn't this amazing? It's after midnight and the place is still packed. I'm sure they could have canceled the game before we even arrived but they knew the Chicago fans would wait. Believe it or not, the game didn't end until two in the morning the next day, and it wasn't even an overtime game. I should add that nobody left the building 'til the game was over."

7. *Proof that Goalies Are Nuts.*
   "My good friend Sugar Jim Henry had played goal for the Rangers and later the Bruins and Blackhawks. Sugar Jim and myself went into partnership in a tourist camp called

The Hockey Haven in Kenora, Ontario. This was sometime in late April, right after the playoffs. A big wind storm had just hit our town and it knocked over a tree that fell on one of our empty tourist cabins. Jim and I were on the roof fixing it when a station wagon pulls up and I look at the guy and his family and say, 'That guy looks familiar.' Well, it was Glenn Hall, who was playing goal for the Blackhawks. My wife knew Glenn's wife and kids, so they went into the house. Meantime, it's raining out but we hollered to Glenn that he should come up and join us. So, he climbed up the ladder, we shook hands and started talking about the playoffs and other hockey things. We went on and on and on about this and that. All of a sudden, the rain came down in torrents, like in the Hollywood movies. There's Hall in his suit, shirt and tie,

By far the best nickname for a sweet goalie belonged to Samuel James Henry who starred for the New York Rangers in the early 1940s. They called him "Sugar Jim" as a New York puckstopper, and later as netminder for the Canadian Army team during World War II.

with water trickling down his face and he's still talkin' hockey with us. Jim looks at him and then looks at me and we burst out laughing. Glenn says, 'What are you guys laughing about?' I looked at the poor rain-soaked guy and said, 'I'll tell you — if you want to know how crazy goaltenders are, we're proving it. We haven't got enough brains to come in out of the rain.' We stood there in the downpour and all broke up. Ever since then, whenever I see Hall, I say, 'Glenn, have you gotten out of the rain yet?'"

8. *The Goalie Scores a Goal.*
"They talk about NHL goalies Billy Smith and Ron Hextall getting credit for scoring a goal in a game but no NHL goaltender can claim that he skated the entire length of the rink to do it. That is, all except me, but I didn't do it in an actual big-league game. It happened during World War II. Like so many other NHL players, I was in the Armed Forces and each branch had its own hockey team comprised of fellows who had been in the pros, be it NHL, AHL or other top leagues. I was in the Canadian Navy and playing goal for their team against the Canadian Army team in Victoria. The goal happened partly because each team had two guys in the penalty box, which meant we were playing three skaters on a side. One of the army players took a shot that hit me high and bounced right out about five yards in front of the net. I looked around and said to myself, 'Geez, I better clear this thing out of the zone.' I skated out and got the puck on my stick and looked around. All three of their players were behind me, and so were our three. 'Wow,' I said, 'I'd better go.' I went for it — straight ahead toward their zone where Art Rice-Jones was in their net. When I looked at him seeing me charging down the ice in full

pads, he seemed scared stiff; he couldn't believe what was coming. Meanwhile, you could have heard a pin drop in the arena, because the fans were in a state of shock, watching a goalie race down the ice on a breakaway. They'd never seen anything like this before. For a split-second, I thought I ought to stop, but then I figured, 'The hell with it, Charlie, go for it.' I kept going and got to a point about 15 feet out and let one go. The puck just made it inside the post by an inch or so and the red light went on. People have asked, 'How come none of the other regulars on their team didn't catch you?' For one thing, I was a real good skater who trained an awful lot and, for another, the guys on their team were absolutely stupefied by the sight of me skating the length of the ice. They didn't know what to make of it or what to do. And that's how I became the first big-league goalie to score a goal in a non-big-league game."

9. *Hockey's First Two-Goalie System.*
"From the very start of the NHL right up until the seasons when I played, starting in 1941 with the Americans, the league employed a one-goalie system. Every club carried one goaltender and if he got seriously hurt in a game, the teams kept a 'house-goalie' who would be called down from the stands and fill in for the rest of the game, if need be. Nobody ever dreamed of keeping two goalies on the bench until after World War II and it happened in a strange way. When the war started, I belonged to the Americans but the club folded after the 1941-42 season, and when the war ended, each team was able to take players from our roster. As luck would have it, the Rangers got me but they also had Sugar Jim Henry, who had played for them when they finished first in 1941-42 and then went off to the war as I did. So now Frank

Boucher, who coached and managed the Rangers, had two first-rank goalies and an unbelievable idea. He decided that he would change goalies *every third shift during every period of the game*. And, lo and behold, that's exactly what we did. Sugar Jim would start and three face-offs later, he'd skate to the bench, I'd take his stick and go right to the crease. Then we'd switch three shifts after that. Since this was such a revolutionary move, some of the more conservative NHL leaders were very unhappy about it. Right up there on the angry list was Toronto's boss, Conn Smythe, who had a running feud with Boucher. They would fight like cats and dogs, so when we played at Maple Leaf Gardens you can imagine Smythe's reaction when he heard what we planned to do. 'To hell with that Smythe,' Boucher said, 'we'll rotate our goalies whether he likes it or not, in front of their big house — and it'll be carried across Canada on Foster Hewitt's broadcast.' True to his word, Frank pulled me after the third face-off and then inserted Sugar Jim and back-and-forth the two of us went. Smythe just about went out of his mind. I mean he couldn't believe it. But Conn had great power in the NHL along with Jim Norris in Detroit. Those two, along with Frank Selke in Montreal, just about controlled the league right after World War II. After what Boucher had done with the two goalies, Smythe squealed to the league, demanding that such a move can't be done. 'We can't have that,' he told the governors and President Clarence Campbell. So, they voted down the Rangers and the two-goalie system ended then and there."

10. *How I Won the Stanley Cup — Almost.*
My biggest regret in hockey is that I never played on a Stanley Cup-winner, although there are very few people around who came closer than I did in 1950. That 1949-50 sea-

son was a humdinger. Toronto had won three straight Cups and Detroit had a tough team with Gordie Howe, Ted Lindsay, Sid Abel, Red Kelly and Harry Lumley in goal. We had some good players too, but we didn't clinch a playoff berth until the very end of the schedule. In order to make it, we had to beat Chicago and we took them 3-2, and just sneaked into the last spot, fourth place. That put us up against the Canadiens in the opening round, and they were heavy favorites. Their goalie, Bill Durnan, had won a slew of Vezina Trophies and Rocket Richard was in his prime along with a lot of other good players. But we got hot at just the right time, which is so important in the playoffs. We whipped them a couple of times and all of a sudden the pendulum swung our way and they began worrying in Montreal that they might blow the whole thing. Durnan wasn't himself and young Gerry McNeil was brought in to replace the master. Well, we beat them four games to one and that set us up against the Red Wings, who had beaten the Maple Leafs in a bitter seven-game series. Now we're in the finals and a strange thing happens — we don't have any games at Madison Square Garden. In those days, the Ringling Brothers Circus would take over the building come hell or high water in April, so we were allowed two 'home games' in a foreign rink, which happened to be Maple Leaf Gardens. Now the finals are underway and everyone figures we're dead because of the opposition and having no games in New York. But we were hot and we surprised the Red Wings. We led them three games to two, but they tied it at three-all, and now it's Game Seven at Olympia in Detroit. We led them 3-2 until late in the second period and, dammit if we didn't get two penalties to two of our best defensemen, Pat Egan and Allan Stanley. Jimmy McFadden tied it up for them (15:57 of the second period) and nobody scored after that through the third period. So it went into the first sudden-death, and that's when we should have won the Cup. Tony Leswick got Lumley way out of the net and had the cage wide open. Our bench had practically emptied in anticipation of the Cup-winner and, already our sticks were all over the ice. But Tony stopped for a split-second just to make sure he put it in and then, all of a sudden, from out of nowhere, Detroit's big defenseman, Black Jack Stewart, skated in and Tony's shot hit his arm and bounced to the side, out of danger. And we had figured that it was all over. Nobody scored in the first overtime and now we're in the second sudden-death and the game was like a see-saw, back-and-forth. Now they get a face-off in our end and George Gee takes it for them, wins the draw and gets the puck to his winger, Pete Babando. He just slapped the puck and, to this day, I don't know whether the puck hit someone and changed direction or what. I looked down and could see it catch the corner and go in, and that was it, the end of it. We didn't win the Cup, but it was an experience. I wound up winning The Hart Trophy, although I got a lot of help from some pretty important guys. But I'll always say that if we had only been able to play a couple of games at Madison Square Garden, we would have won the Stanley Cup."

THE TWO BEST RATS IN HOCKEY HISTORY

1. *Harry Westwick.* The only "Rat" in hockey's Hall of Fame, Westwick had the distinction of being a first-class goaltender and a rover. He broke into pro hockey with the Ottawa Silver Seven in 1895 as a netminder but switched to rover in his rookie season and starred at that position for the next dozen seasons. Harry not only averaged better than a goal a game but played on three consecutive Stanley Cup-winners with the Seven. He was the first star to be nicknamed Rat.

2. *Ken Linseman.* His opponents have often said that this contemporary Rat was aptly named. Originally a member of the WHA Birmingham Bulls, Linesman joined the Philadelphia Flyers in 1977 as compensation for the Rangers' signing of Fred Shero as coach. Notorious as an instigator who rarely dropped his stick to battle, Linesman nevertheless was a very competent center whose NHL career spanned more than a decade.

SIX ZANIES ON ICE AND THEIR STUNTS

1. *Charlie Conacher.* He's the Hall of Famer who once held teammate Baldy Cotton by the ankles upside-down from a 12th floor window of Manhattan's Lincoln Hotel. The reason? Charlie was miffed because Baldy had been bugging him about not passing enough the night before. When Cotton finally apologized, Conacher hauled him to safety.

2. *Gilles Gratton.* This delightful French-Canadian wasn't nicknamed "Grattoony The Looney" for nothing. As a member of the WHA's Toronto Toros, he once streaked — as in completely nude, not as in winning streak — except for a pair of skates around Maple Leaf Gardens during a scrimmage.

3. *Eddie Shack.* Nicknamed "The Entertainer" — also "Clear The Deck" — Shack had a distracting habit of bodychecking his own men as well as the opposition. One night, after Shack had dropped Maple Leafs teammate Bert Olmstead, Dirty Bertie grabbed a hunk of Shack's jersey on the bench and said, "L-E-A-F-S — I'm on your team."

4. *Eddie Shore.* The Bruins' immortal thought of himself as a skating Lionel Barrymore (or John Gielgud, if you will)

and liked to skate on the ice at the start of some Boston Garden games wearing a toreador's cape across the shoulder. The band would play "Hail To The Chief" as a valet followed him to center ice where the butler would take the cape from his shoulders allowing the game to begin.

The most injured superstar of all time is a category topped by the immortal Eddie Shore, who endured more than 200 stitches around his head and once had his ear sewn back on after it was nearly sliced off by an enemy stick. Shore is shown here as a member of the New York Americans along with coach Red Dutton.

5. *Eddie Shore (same guy, only now as off-the-wall owner of the Springfield Indians minor league team.)* After his goalie Don "Nipper" O'Hearn's wife had twin girls, Shore met privately with his netminder and declared, "If you'd come to me, you'd have had boys." O'Hearn couldn't understand the logic until Shore explained, "I'd have shown you how to screw by the moon!"

6. *Wilf Cude.* This shell-shocked goalie got angry at his wife after she had placed a too-tough steak on the table. Cude took the T-bone ad hurled it across the room against the far wall. "From the time it hit the wall," Cude remembered, "to the time it slipped to the floor, I knew I had had enough of goaltending and quit then and there."

THE THREE BEST LINES WITH NICKNAMES

1. *The Kraut Line.* Childhood chums in Kitchener, Ontario, center Milt Schmidt, left wing Woody Dumart and right wing Bobby Bauer were teen stars in their hometown. Dumart and Schmidt originally played together — without Bauer — for Kitchener in the Ontario Hockey League, a Junior circuit for players under 21. Dumart made his debut with the Bruins in 1936-37. Bauer gained early stardom while attending St. Michael's College in Toronto. In 1934-35, Bauer graduated to Kitchener in the OHL and then teamed with Schmidt and Dumart. Since Kitchener had a sizeable population of German-Canadians, the trio was dubbed the Sauerkraut Line, which eventually was shortened to Kraut Line after they graduated to the NHL. Schmidt became a Bruin a year after his pals, and once united they became the scourge of the pre-World War II NHL, starting in 1937-38. Just when the line had reached its peak in 1941-42, the three enlisted in the Royal Canadian Air Force. They returned to the NHL in 1945-46. Bauer retired a year later, but made one more appearance in 1951-52 to play at Boston Garden in a "night" honoring The Kraut Line. He scored a goal and an assist on that occasion, then permanently retired. Dumart remained a Bruin through the 1953-54 season, after starring in Boston's 1953 playoff upset of the vaunted Detroit Red

Wings. Schmidt hung up his Bruins skates a year later to become coach of the team.

2. *The Kid Line.* When impresario Conn Smythe organized the Toronto Maple Leafs — originally the Toronto St. Patricks — in the late 1920s, he put together a line comprised of right wing Charlie Conacher, center Joe Primeau and left wing Harold Cotton. Just before Christmas 1929, Smythe made the move that would alter hockey history. He pulled Cotton off the line and inserted Busher Jackson in his place on left wing. Hockey's first and most renowned Kid Line was born. Success was as dramatic as a volcanic eruption. Toronto defeated the Blackhawks, Canadiens and Montreal Maroons right after Christmas and went undefeated until January 23 of the new year. The Kid Line remained intact through the early '30s. Conacher owned the booming shot, Primeau was the sophisticated playmaker and Jackson, according to Leafs aide Frank Selke, "could pivot on a dime, stickhandle through an entire team without giving up the puck, and shoot like a bullet from either forehand or backhand. His backhand was the best I ever saw." Primeau retired in 1936, Jackson in 1944 as a Bruin, and Conacher in 1941, after a fling with the New York Americans.

3. *Punch Line.* It began with left wing Toe Blake's arrival in Montreal with the Canadiens in 1935 and progressed in 1940 when Elmer Lach was signed as a Habs center. At first Blake was used on a unit with Johnny Quilty and Joe Benoit, but coach Dick Irvin soon changed that with the insertion of Lach at center. The Canadiens were improving with Blake leading the way, but they didn't reach maturity as a championship club until 1943-44 when Irvin inserted young, fiery Maurice Richard on right wing with

Blake and Lach. The trio finished one-two-three (Lach, Blake, Richard) in scoring on the team and the Canadiens finished first and capped the campaign by winning the Stanley Cup. The Punch Line became one of the classiest units in the NHL and guided Montreal to another Stanley Cup in 1946. Blake scored 29 regular season goals that year, but then began a decline in his playing fortunes. He scored only nine goals in 1947-48, a year in which the Canadiens missed the playoffs, and then made his exit from the NHL. Lach, who played 13 seasons for the Habs, finished his career in 1954, while the immortal Rocket remained a Canadiens leader until his retirement in 1960.

THE TEN CRAZIEST NON-1994 ENCOUNTERS OF THE STANLEY CUP

1. It was kicked into the Rideau Canal by celebrating members of the Ottawa Silver Seven in 1905, led by Harry Smith. A day later, Smith remembered where he had punted the trophy and retrieved it in the bone-dry bed.

2. A cleaning woman at Rice Photo Studios in Montreal thought it would be a neat planter for geraniums after the Canadiens had left it there following a team photo shoot.

3. Montreal fan Ken Kilander hoisted it out of a glass case in Chicago Stadium and walked out of the arena with the stolen Cup before being apprehended.

4. Bryan Trottier and his wife Nicki took the Cup to bed with them after the New York Islanders won the 1980 championship.

5. New York Rangers president John Reed Kilpatrick burned the Madison Square Garden mortgage in the mug following the Blueshirts' 1940 Stanley Cup victory.

6. Guy Lafleur packed it in the trunk of his car and, without anyone's knowledge, drove it to his Thurso, Quebec hometown where it was displayed on his lawn. Panicking Cup trustees thought the trophy had been stolen.

7. Islanders left wing Clark Gillies used it as a dog-food tray after the Isles won the 1981 title and his mutt enjoyed several slurps of Alpo out of the silverware.

8. The Canadiens were taking it to the home of owner Leo Dandurand following a 1924 playoff triumph when the auto carrying the mug suffered a flat tire. For some reason, the players hauled the Cup out of the car and placed it on the side of the road. Once the flat was fixed, the boys took off for the celebration but forgot the poor symbol of their championship. Only later did they realize their oversight, and hustled back to the place of flat-fixing to retrieve the lonely Cup.

9. Mario Lemieux delivered it to his Pittsburgh mansion where Penguins teammates alternated leaping into the swimming pool accompanied by Lord Stanley's gift. After several experiments, Phil Bourque declared, "It can't swim."

10. Rangers left wing Lynn Patrick mistook Stanley for an outhouse and urinated in the bowl, whereupon other teammates followed with their piddles.

The Ten Craziest 1994 Encounters of the Stanley Cup

1. *June 14.* Esa Tikkanen leads a conga line while holding it out of the Manhattan saloon Auction House, down 89th Street to the East River. Then Mark Messier takes it to an East Side strip joint, Scores, where customers touch the 32-pound symbol of hockey supremacy instead of the dancers.

2. *June 16.* National, a Russian night club in the Brighton Beach section of Brooklyn hosts the Cup, thanks to defenseman Sergei Zubov. "We not fill Cup with borscht!" insists club manager Simon Maklin.

3. *June 17.* Stanley leads a ticker tape parade up Broadway and stops at City Hall where Mayor Rudy Giuliani's hockey-mad eight-year-old son, Andrew, embraces it before a throng estimated at more than a million celebrants.

4. *June 20.* Actress Brooke Shields and New York Yankee outfielder Daryl Boston are among many party-goers with Nick Kypreos and Brian Leetch at the China Club nighterie. Actor Mickey Rourke is the only patron who will not pose with Stanley.

5. *June 21.* At Yankee Stadium, a press credential is actually made out in the name of Stanley Cup. The mug watches the Yankee game from George Steinbrenner's box. That same day, Messier carries Stanley to Columbia-Presbyterian Hospital, where 13-year-old Rangers fan Brian Bluver is suffering from cardiomyopathy (a disease of the heart) and awaiting a heart transplant. "When Brian saw the Cup, he smiled for the first time in seven weeks," says his father, Bill. "He was too weak to speak,

yet I'd never seen him so happy. A week-and-a-half later Brian had 11th-hour heart surgery. I think The Cup was a tremendous part of helping him stay alive."

6. *July 1.* Horse-fancier Ed Olczyk drives the oversized trophy to Belmont racetrack, fills it with oats and feeds Kentucky Derby-winner Go For Gin out of Stanley's jaws.

7. *July 2.* Kypreos and Brian Noonan are featured with the Cup on "MTV Prime Time Beach House" where they chuckle as Stanley is stuffed with raw clams and oysters. During the show, Noonan denies he used the Cup as a rolling pin to make muffins. The mammoth silverware was dressed in a T-shirt, baseball cap and false moustache.

8. *July 7.* Miller The Driller, a.k.a. Dr. Irwin Miller, the Rangers team dentist, hosts the Cup in his office in White Plains, New York, after which it is hustled over to the Sunshine Pizza Lounge by Bruce Lifrieri. After a fan kisses Stanley, Lifrieri observes, "God only knows whose lips have been on that thing."

9. *July 8.* Club equipment manager Joe Murphy embraces Stanley at the Providence Rest Nursing home in his native Bronx. The host nuns pose with a baby sitting in the Cup. It then is put on a pedestal and swaddled in blue velvet. "The Cup is not the Holy Grail," says Sister Joanne, "but it is something very, very special."

10. *July 11.* Stanley needs a vacation and is driven by Kypreos and Lifrieri to a resort on Long Island. "It's not often you get quiet time with the Cup," Lifrieri reflects at poolside at five in the morning. Kypreos then intercepts the prize and concludes, "See you later — we're going to bed."

Hall-of-Fame Goalie Glenn Hall's Seven Memorable Moments

1. *Winning the Stanley Cup but losing the Cup-winning party.* "The Blackhawks had only won two Stanley Cups — in 1934 and 1938 — when we were going for the prize in 1961. We were leading the Red Wings three games to two in the 1961 finals with Game Six at Detroit's Olympia. It was April 22, already spring, and the deal was that if we won it that night, our owners would fly the team right back to Chicago for a big party at one of the classy hotels. Detroit got a one-goal lead in the first, but we bounced back with two in the second and wrapped it up with three in the third to win the game 5-1, and the Cup. I always have said that the highlight of my career was just playing in the National Hockey League because I enjoyed the game so much, but playing on that one Stanley Cup-winner topped everything. After the game, we were all ready to fly back to Chicago for the huge celebration but, believe it or not, there was a snowstorm in Detroit that night and by the time we got to the airport they said that all planes were grounded. So we went back to our hotel, which was an old place called The Leland. The team was only able to rent a small suite but we had our makeshift party there, although it really wasn't the Cup-winning party that it was supposed to be. That came later after the snow stopped falling."

2. *Putting on a mask for the first time after having played 502 consecutive games without wearing a face protector.* "I remember this vividly because it took place in New York at what was then the new Madison Square Garden. This was in the late 1960s at a time when a lot of the players started using the curved sticks and slapping the puck

like crazy. A lot of the goalies already had been wearing a mask; in fact Jacques Plante already had been using one for almost ten years. I finally gave in and decided to give it a try against New York, so I put it on and went out on the Garden ice. Everything was okay for a while. One of the hardest shooters in the league was Vic Hadfield of the Rangers, and on this night he skated over the blue line and served one up on me. With the kind of unrestricted banana-blade they had in those days, a guy like Hadfield could get the puck to come in like a zooming knuckleball. I watched it come at me, drop and then it looked to me like it was going behind the net. Instead, it dropped into the top corner. I didn't like that and I must have been incensed, because then I had a couple of arguments with the referee. One thing led to another and before you knew it, I was kicked out of the game. Afterwards one of the reporters asked me about the incident and I said, 'Every time I wear a mask I get kicked out of the game.' Which was true. I wore the mask that one time and I was given the hook. By the way, I wore it for two-and-a-half more years, but never felt comfortable with the protection."

3. *The shot style changes from wrist-only to slapper.*
"When I first came into the NHL during the 1952-53 season, there were basically two kinds of shots faced by goaltenders. The most common was the wrist shot, but a lot of players, especially Rocket Richard, used the backhander. Then Bernie Geoffrion came along just about when I became a regular and he introduced the slapshot. At first Boom Boom was the only one to use it on a consistent basis and, let me tell you, he really opened a lot of eyes. Pretty soon, other sharpshooters picked up on it. Andy Bathgate of the Rangers was one, and then our own Bobby Hull. By the time Bobby had perfected his slap-

shot, it was the hardest shot I ever looked at, no question — even as hard as anybody shooting today. Of course, my problem was that I had to face Hull's shot every day in practice when we weren't playing. For protection, they had made a little plastic face mask just for use in scrimmages. It wasn't much protection because it seemed more like cardboard than anything, but I didn't want to lose an eye in practice and, as a goalie, I was very eye-conscious. Much later on, I realized that it would be stupid to play without a mask in a regular game."

4. *The best defensemen in front of him and best goalies on the other side.* "I always wanted to have defensemen who were complementary to a goalkeeper and who were not necessarily the best all-round defensemen in the league. One such player was Bob Goldham, who I played with briefly in Detroit. Goldham was one of the best puck-blocking defensemen in the league. Then there was Al Arbour who I worked with in Chicago when we won the Stanley Cup and later with the St. Louis Blues. Al wasn't a flashy type, but he took care of business and was unbelievable at shot-blocking. I really enjoyed and appreciated his game. Pierre Pilote was our top defenseman in Chicago and a Norris Trophy-winner. He was terrific at moving the puck. Last, but certainly not least, there's Doug Harvey, who played his best hockey in Montreal but still had something left when we teamed up with the Blues. Doug was an absolute quality defenseman with terrific instincts and know-how. The best goalie I've ever seen was Terry Sawchuk, who preceded me in Detroit and then went to Boston after I became a Red Wing. Then there was Charlie Rayner, who never really played with great Ranger teams but won the Hart Trophy in 1950. Rayner was terrific in my estimation."

5. *Alternating in goal with another Hall-of-Famer, Jacques Plante.* "I joined the St. Louis Blues in 1967 after I was taken in the expansion draft from Chicago. That was the Blues first season in the league. Next year, St. Louis drafted Plante and we became teammates for the 1968-69 season. Having been around so long, I knew Jacques, but never as a teammate. I had been told in advance that he was difficult to get along with, but I never had any problems with him, although he certainly was different. If he wanted to talk, I talked to him and if he didn't want to talk, we didn't talk. I could appreciate that in anybody, not just a goalkeeper. But we had a great couple of years together and when you think about it, if you had combined our ages at the time, it would have come to about 80 years old, so we were certainly past our prime. In our first year together, Jacques had a 1.96 goals against average and mine was 2.17 and we won the Vezina Trophy. I had eight shutouts and he had five. We had one more year together and then he went on to Toronto. In those two seasons we did pretty well for ourselves, although I must admit that the Scotty Bowman-defensive style complemented the goaltenders. We took the credit for a lot of things our teammates were doing for us and making it so much easier. Defensemen like Al Arbour were taking away the rebounds and that helped extend our careers. Of course, we still knew how to play, but we just weren't as quick as we once had been."

6. *The Annual Glenn Hall Paint-the-Barn Ploy.* "In the mid-1960s, after I had been around the NHL quite a while, I occasionally would think about packing it in. At about that time, this story — that has almost become legend — began to make the rounds. Basically it had to do with our barn and the fact that I always seemed to be right in the midst of painting it just when training camp started. The writers said

I used that as an alibi to avoid coming to camp. As I remember it, the whole gambit began when the Blackhawks sent me the usual training camp information in the mail. I suppose there was some stuff that I should have responded to but I just ignored it and didn't show up, and that's when they began wondering what was happening with me. In those days you didn't make an announcement about retiring, but when our general manager Tommy Ivan got in touch with me, I told him that I had retired. I was only in my early 30s at the time and my goals against average was usually below 2.50, which was quite good, so Ivan wouldn't have any part of me retiring. But it happened that I was painting the barn and I was thinking about retiring but then, all of a sudden, I was being offered more money so I figured that I couldn't afford not to be playing. So, I finished painting the barn and then showed up with the Hawks. From that point on in my career, whenever I was a bit late for camp, they'd say that 'Glenn is painting his barn.' "

7. *Throwing up before every single game.* "It may have seemed unusual to some outsiders, but I simply felt that I played better if I had vomited before the game. I always felt that if you're capable of playing well, anything less than that level is unacceptable, so I built myself up to that degree. It [throwing up] forced me into being ready."

Four Reasons Why Alexander Daigle Is the Biggest Build-Up to a Letdown of the 1990s

1. He received a $12.25 million contract, which means he's overpaid by at least $11 million.

2. During Daigle's rookie season, 1993-94, the following freshmen placed higher than him in the Calder Trophy balloting: Martin Brodeur, Jason Arnott, Mikael Renberg, Alexei Yashin, Chris Osgood, Sandis Ozolinsh and Derek Plante.

3. He hasn't a clue about backchecking.

4. He was supposed to be the cornerstone of the Senators franchise, but may merely be the stone that pulls it underwater.

FOUR PEOPLE WHO WOULD RATHER VISIT LOWER SLOBOVIA THAN UPPER QUEBEC CITY

1. Eric Lindros

2. Brett Lindros

3. Bonnie Lindros

4. Carl Lindros

THE BIGGEST TOP DRAFT PICK-FLOP TO BECOME A PLAYERS' AGENT

In 1983, the Minnesota North Stars selected Brian Lawton ahead of Pat LaFontaine, Steve Yzerman, Tom Barrasso and Cam Neely as the number one overall pick in the Entry Draft. A product of Mount St.Charles High School in Woonsocket, Rhode Island, Lawton evolved as one of the most disappointing top choices since the draft's inception. The problem wasn't Brian's; it was a matter of the North Stars miscalculating and thereby placing far too much pressure on the lad. "If I had been taken in the third round," says Lawton, "I'd have been a hero. But there are a lot of expectations built into being a Number One. And because I wasn't a star, I was under scrutiny. But I did play about 500 NHL games. I'm proud of my career." While playing for the San Jose Sharks in 1992, Lawton became the team's player representative during the 1992 players' strike. It was then that he became interested in the business side of hockey and, upon his retirement, became a Minneapolis-based player agent.

The Three Most Significant Players' Strikes

1. *Hamilton Tigers Player Walkoff.*
   In 1924-25 the Hamilton Tigers had one of the NHL's better teams, but several of its players became disenchanted with the pay scale as related to a change in the playoff format. Tigers ace Red Green drew attention to the fact that he had signed a two-year contract the previous season calling for a 24-game schedule. Noting that he had already played 30 games and was being asked to play more, he and his teammates demanded an extra $200 each. NHL President Frank Calder refused to give in to the strikers and ruled that the Stanley Cup semi-final winner would represent the league in the Cup final if the Tigers didn't return to the ice. The players were adamant in their stand, whereupon the Montreal Canadiens defeated Toronto 3-2 and 2-0 to advance against the Victoria Cougars for the Cup. (Victoria won the series three games to one). The Tigers were suspended in April

and fined $200 each. Then the team was sold to a New York group headed by bootlegging baron Big Bill Dwyer for $75,000 and appeared in 1925-26 as the New York Americans. Among the Tiger players who were reinstated and made the jump to the Amerks, besides Red and Shorty Green, were Billy Burch, Ken Randall, Alec McKinnon, Charlie Langlois, Mickey Roach, Edmond Bouchard and goalie Vernon (Jumpin' Jake) Forbes. The schedule was again extended — to 36 games — but there was no more strike talk.

2. *The Anti-Shore Springfield Rebellion.*
The American Hockey League's Springfield Indians had been owned by Hall-of-Famer Eddie Shore since before World War II. A character who would make both Simon Legree and Captain Bligh seem mild by comparison, Shore was notoriously tough on his players to the point of being brutal at times. During the post-World War II years and into the 1950s and early 1960s, Shore was able to get away with his insensitive tactics. But as the union movement in other professional sports began gaining headway, hockey players began to think about improving their conditions. Finally, in the mid-1960s, a group of Indians, fed up with Shore's tactics, asked Toronto attorney Alan Eagleson to intervene on their behalf. Eagleson encouraged the players to call a strike, which they did. Despite Shore's power within the AHL, he was removed from domination of the Springfield club because of "highly unorthodox" treatment of his players and was eventually forced to sell the team to the Los Angeles Kings, who had entered the NHL for the 1967-68 expansion season. The acclaim Eagleson obtained from the settlement helped boost him to prominence and "The Eagle" became the first executive director of the NHL Players' Association.

3. *The 1992 Pre-Playoff NHL Uprising.*
Throughout the lengthy NHLPA stewardship of Alan Eagleson, the union and league ownership existed in a rather pleasant alliance. Eagleson was on most friendly terms with NHL President John Ziegler as well as league board chairman Bill Wirtz. But by the 1991-92 season, several player agents had suggested to their clients that The Eagle was not fully representing them and an anti-Eagleson movement took hold within the rank-and-file stickhandlers' group. When the players replaced Eagleson with former agent Bob Goodenow, the union took a stand that was considerably tougher than it had been before and this was manifested early in 1992 when negotiations between Goodenow and Ziegler became earnest over a new Collective Bargaining Agreement. Despite intensive meetings in Manhattan, an agreement could not be reached and the players called a strike, despite only a handful of games remaining in the season. The ten-day walkout was filled with recriminations and the distinct possibility that the playoffs would have to be cancelled. At a point just when it seemed no deal was possible, a group of players led by Wayne Gretzky and Mark Messier prevailed on the NHLPA to hammer out a settlement and this was finally done on a Friday night at the Plaza Hotel. The remaining games were played as were the playoffs. However, the major victim of the settlement was Ziegler who soon was forced to leave his post. By contrast, Goodenow emerged stronger than ever, as did his Players' Association.

The Best and Worst of Brian Sutter as Coach

1. *The 180-Degree Verbal Turn.* When Sutter coached the St. Louis Blues in 1991-92, his twin brothers, Ron and Rich, played for him. Sutter was sensitive to criticism that he was guilty of nepotism and one day was asked about complimenting the twins. "I never compliment them," Sutter snapped. But a reporter quickly retorted that he certainly did lavish such praise, whereupon Brian shot back, "Why shouldn't I?"

2. *A Sweet Gesture for an Aging Warrior.* During the 1991-92 campaign, Sutter and veteran defenseman Lee Norwood frequently clashed. With one game remaining on the schedule, Norwood required just a single contest on ice to qualify for 50 games and a $20,000 bonus. Brian obliged by playing Lee who got his extra 20 Gs.

From the Penthouse to the Outhouse to the Broadcast Booth

No hockey personality has endured a more up-and-down life on and off the ice than Derek Sanderson. The Boston Bruins center, who starred on Beantown's 1970 and 1972 Stanley Cup champions, reached his peak in 1972 when he signed the fattest contract ever offered a team player in the world — $2.65 million. The new World Hockey Association team in Philadelphia signed Turk, who promptly bought a 28-room house and a new Rolls Royce.

But the WHA club hardly lasted and Sanderson's career began a slow but steady decline. By 1984 Derek was broke, couldn't walk and had become a victim of alcohol and drugs. The CBS program "60 Minutes" zeroed in on Derek's plight and soon his hockey friends, including Bobby Orr, steered him to rehabilitation.

Sanderson eventually recovered enough to become a broadcast analyst for Bruins games and was actively involved in the Boston community as a speaker who addresses youngsters on the perils of booze and pills.

In order to regain the ability to walk, Derek required several operations, the first three of which were unsuccessful. "Dr. Allan Gross [one of the Toronto Blue Jays' doctors] practically saved my life," Sanderson asserted. "He took a look at me after the three other operations and did two operations to replace my hips. Some people say I walk like Charlie Chaplin, but I'm walking and I love it!"

GLEN SONMOR'S FAVORITE BILL GOLDTHORPE STORY

Anyone who played with or against Bill Goldthorpe in the mid-1970s will admit that he was among the wildest characters ever to skate on a sheet of ice. *Ottawa Sun* columnist Earl McRae once said this of Goldie: "Goldthorpe joyously beat up players in dressing rooms, in penalty boxes, on the ice, in the streets, in bars, in homes, and that's only his teammates; he did the same to guys on the other teams. He'd been shot at, knifed, crowbar whacked, run over by a car, and he kept coming back for more, totally fearless." Goldthorpe played briefly in the World Hockey Association for the Minnesota Fighting Saints, Baltimore Blades, San Diego Mariners as well as innumerable International, Eastern and American League clubs. When he played for Minnesota, ex-NHLer Glen Sonmor was the coach in a playoff game with the Houston Aeros. At the time Gordie

Howe skated for Houston alongside his sons, Mark and Marty. Howe was notorious for his toughness and few players dared challege Mister Hockey. But Ogie was an exception. Here's how Sonmor tells it:

"Ogie wasn't really playing so he would sit on the bench and yell out at Gordie Howe: 'Gordie, you old (censored), you're all washed-up. If they let me out there, I'll rip your (censored) head off.'

"Howe looked over and we had a little guy named Keith Christiansen sitting next to Goldthorpe, and he yelled out, 'That wasn't me, Gordie, honest, that wasn't me who said it.'

"Finally, there was a fracas and Goldthorpe got out of there and he tried to get at Howe, but he couldn't. So he yelled at him, 'Gordie, you won't play forever and when you quit, I'm gonna kick the crap out of your two kids.'"

MOST HONEST ADMISSION OF FIBBERY BY AN NHL COACH

During the 1993 Stanley Cup playoffs, Los Angeles Kings leader Barry Melrose took considerable heat from the media for being secretive about injuries to his key players, especially Wayne Gretzky. Finally, Melrose explained, "I'm always honest with you guys — unless I'm lying!"

GARY BETTMAN'S TEN BEST MOVES SINCE BECOMING COMMISSIONER

1. *Studying*. The new NHL boss carefully read page 69 of *The All-Time Book of Hockey Lists*, which delineated predecessor John Ziegler's "Eight Biggest Mistakes as NHL President."

2. *Showing up.* Bettman has visited more arenas and seen more NHL games in two years than Ziegler did in 16 seasons.

3. *Media Relations.* From Day One, Bettman has become the most accessible leader the NHL has known and always advises journalists, "Call me Gary."

4. *Public Relations.* Whereas Ziegler had closed the league's New York P.R. office, Bettman not only re-opened it, but has more than quadrupled its size.

5. *The Dale Hunter-Pierre Turgeon Incident.* After the Capitals headhunter cheap-shotted the Islanders ace from behind in the 1993 playoffs, Bettman responded by suspending Hunter for the first 21 games of the 1993-94 season, one of the most severe penalties ever invoked. Except in New York, most critics lauded the decision as pleasingly tough.

6. *L'Affaire Gil Stein.* Interim NHL president Gil Stein altered the format of the Hall of Fame voting. Many journalists accused Stein of rigging the format to enable himself to be inducted. Bettman quickly convened an independent two-member panel to examine the case. They ruled against Stein in an elaborate report which received high praise across the board.

7. *Ottawa's Messy Finish.* A printed (later denied) comment by Senators leader Bruce Firestone suggested that at the end of the 1992-93 season, Ottawa played less than its best in order to secure the first draft pick, which would eventually be Alexandre Daigle. Once again, Bettman drafted his two-man panel who conducted an intensive probe. They found no gross misdeeds, but their work against was warmly approved.

8. *Realignment.* Bettman won quick approval from his ownership to alter the traditional Smythe, Norris, Adams, Patrick Division names and change the playoff format to allow for more widespread fan interest. The new arrangement went into effect during the 1993-94 campaign and inspired more interest than the previous system.

9. *The European Pact.* After decades in which the NHL and the International Ice Hockey Federation remained at arm's-length — if that close — Bettman cemented a new treaty with the IIHF during the summer of 1994. Among its features is an agreement whereby the NHL will pay transfer fees for Europeans and the promise to work together for the formation of a Pan-Europe Super League.

10. *Keenan's Team-Hopping.* When Stanley Cup-winning coach Mike Keenan announced that the New York Rangers had broken their contract with him following the 1994 championship, Keenan declared himself a free agent. However, the Rangers claimed that he had broken his pact and the Detroit Red Wings also were accused of tampering for Keenan's services. Bettman acted swiftly, convened a hearing of all parties and handed out penalties that appeared to be rather stiff. However, the Blues wound up getting Keenan as coach, while the Rangers obtained potential superstar Petr Nedved and the Red Wings simply were given a wrist-slap. Under the circumstances, all parties were satisfied and the messy event was dispensed with almost as quickly as it erupted.

Five Mistakes by Bettman

1. Suspensions — no clear rule.

2. Playoff format — lucky pairing in first year.

3. 2-3-2 in playoff.

4. Marketability — Jeremy Roenick isn't in a commercial yet.

5. Continued growth of neutral site games.

The Five Best Watsons

1. *Harry Watson.* Nominated for The Hockey Hall of Fame in 1994, the big Saskatoon native lasted 16 years in the bigs, starting with the New York Americans in 1941-42 and ending with the 1956-57 Chicago Blackhawks. Although he played briefly for the Detroit Red Wings in 1942-43, Harry's best years were spent in Toronto from 1946 through 1955. He played on Stanley Cup-winners in 1947, 1948, 1949 and 1951 as left wing. Watson's most successful line found him working with center Syl Apps and right wing Bill Ezinicki during the 1947-48 Leafs' march to first place and the Cup. Quiet and tough, big Harry owned a superb shot and superior savvy.

2. *Phil Watson.* One of the most colorful characters, both as a player and later a coach, Fiery Phil, as he was affectionately known, is best remembered as center on the New York Rangers' 1940 Stanley Cup-winning team. It was Watson, the center, who set up his right wing, Bryan

Hextall, for the overtime goal in Game Six which clinched the title for New York. During World War II, Watson was "loaned" to the Montreal Canadiens for the 1943-44 season while he worked in a defense plant. He returned to the Rangers the following season and completed his career on Broadway in 1947-48. After a minor league coaching stint, Phil was hired as Rangers head coach in 1955-56 and orchestrated three straight playoff teams, but no Cup-winners. Argumentative and often difficult on his players, Watson was fired in 1960 a season after his club had folded abysmally in the final weeks of the 1958-59 season, blowing a playoff berth to Toronto on the final night of the season. Phil spent one season coaching the Boston Bruins in 1961-62 and had two stints in the World Hockey Association with Philadelphia and Vancouver before retiring from the game.

3. *Bryan Watson.* As versatile a skater as ever played, Bugsy was equally at home on defense or the attack. In a career that spanned more than 15 years in the NHL, this undersized hitter played for the Montreal Canadiens, Detroit Red Wings, Oakland Seals, Pittsburgh Penguins, St. Louis Blues, Washington Capitals and Edmonton Oilers. He started in 1963 as a Hab and was still going strong in 1979 with Edmonton. In 1966, Bobby Hull described Bugsy as "Superpest" for his role of shadowing the Blackhawks star when he was on the ice. At the time that he jumped to the World Hockey Association Oilers in 1979, Watson owned the NHL career record for penalty minutes with a total of 2,212. As a Penguin in 1971-72, Watson led the league with 212 penalty minutes. Bugsy is best remembered for his effervescence and knack for extracting every ounce of ability out of his not-so-formidable fuselage.

4. *Joe Watson.* A key member of the Philadelphia Flyers' Stanley Cup-winners in 1974 and 1975, this solid defenseman played hard but unobtrusively in a career that began in 1964-65 with the Boston Bruins and concluded in 1978-79 with the Colorado Rockies. Although not known for his scoring prowess, Joe totalled 30 points in 1976-77.

5. *Jim Watson.* Joe's kid brother, Jimmy, played an almost identical game to Joe's efficient style. A career Flyer, Jimmy arrived in Philadelphia in 1972-73 and became a full-time backliner a year later. He was particularly effective in the 1975 playoffs, collecting nine points in 17 games. The younger Watson finished his career in 1981-82 on Broad Street.

THE TWO BEST CAT GOALTENDERS

1. *Felix Potvin.* The Toronto Maple Leafs assured themselves of netminding success through the 1990s when they drafted this French Canadian with the unorthodox style. Although he's too young to remember the original comic strip after which he is nicknamed, Potvin can trace his sobriquet to "Felix The Cat" of cartoon fame.

2. *Emile Francis.* This "Cat" is named after the one who has nine-lives. Unlike Felix Potvin, "Cat" Francis never was a particularly accomplished goaltender, although he managed to hang around the National Hockey League for a decade. Emile "The Cat" broke with the Chicago Blackhawks in 1946 and moved over to the New York Rangers in 1948. His last big-league season was 1951-52, after which he played in the minors and then went into coaching and managing. He had quite a few lives in that area as well.

The best quote about hockey's uncertain nature comes from Emile "The Cat" Francis, who played goal for the Blackhawks and Rangers, then coached and managed the New Yorkers. When something unusual would happen on the rink, The Cat would purr, "Hockey is a slippery game — it's played on ice!"

THE TEN BEST HOCKEY CENTERS IN NORTH AMERICA

1. *Toronto.* The newspapers — *Sun, Star, Globe and Mail* — have the best NHL coverage, Maple Leaf Gardens is Canada's ice cathedral, and the magnificent Hockey Hall of Fame is situated in the Queen City. In addition, several key NHL offices, including the officiating bureau, are housed there.

2. *Montreal.* The Canadiens have the best tradition, more Stanley Cup-winners, marvelous French-language newspaper coverage and the most knowledgeable fans in the world.

3. *New York-New Jersey Metropolitan Area.* No place in the world boasts three National Hockey League teams (Rangers, Islanders, Devils) in such close proximity and with such delicious inter-county rivalries.

4. *Chicago.* There are no more dedicated, vocal or intense fans than those in the Windy City even if they now are housed in the new, antiseptic United Center (alias Chicago Stadium II). But the organ remains a vital aspect of the ambience.

5. *Quebec.* Not only is hockey the only game in town, but it is worshipped with a religious fervor by the only 100 per cent francophone audience in the league. Le Colisée not only has a dandy aura, but the best hot dogs in the NHL as well.

6. *Boston.* The legacy of Eddie Shore, Frankie Brimsek and Bobby Orr is maintained by the oldest U.S. franchise. Soon-to-be-demolished Boston Garden is a one-of-a-kind relic. Its replacement, Shawmut Center, won't come close for nostalgia purposes but might be infested with fewer rats.

7. *Vancouver.* A new arena is on the way for a town that has enjoyed a hockey renaissance with the Canucks trip to the 1994 Stanley Cup finals. Tony Gallagher's column in *The Province* has some of the best gossip in Canada. A classy front office hasn't hurt, either.

8. *Philadelphia.* Despite a spate of non-playoff teams in the early 1990s, The Spectrum has remained filled. Thanks to Bob Clarke's return as president and the presence of Eric Lindros, the mania should remain.

9. *Winnipeg.* There's always hockey weather in this quintessential hockey town that has produced more pros per population than any city in the world. If the Jets ever became contenders...Wow!

10. *Southern California.* Wayne Gretzky turned Lotusland into hockey paradise and now The Mighty Ducks of Anaheim — just the other side of Los Angeles — have made this a veritable puck hub. Having Disney on board hasn't hurt a bit.

NATIONAL HOCKEY LEAGUE PLAYERS WHO HAVE BEEN NAMED TO THE ORDER OF CANADA

(The Order of Canada is the nation's pre-eminent system of honoring those who have made meaningful achievements on all levels, from local to international.)

1. Syl Apps, captain and center of Toronto Stanley Cup-winners, 1942, 1947 and 1948.

2. Jean Beliveau, captain and center of Montreal Canadiens Stanley Cup winners, and later a club vice-president.

3. Toe Blake, left wing and later coach of Montreal Canadiens who, among other things, won five straight Stanley Cups between 1956-60.

4. Bob Clarke, captain and center of Philadelphia Flyers Stanley Cup-winners in 1974 and 1975, and now president of the Flyers.

5. Phil Esposito, Boston Bruins and New York Rangers scoring star, hero of the 1972 Team Canada-Russia series and currently general manager of the Tampa Bay Lightning.

6. Wayne Gretzky, hockey's foremost contemporary scorer and ambassador.

7. Gordie Howe, the greatest all-round hockey player of modern time.

8. Bobby Hull, star of Chicago's 1961 Stanley Cup-winners, and one of the hardest shooters in history, as well as World Hockey Association pioneer.

9. Guy Lafleur, spearhead of the Montreal Canadiens club that won four straight Stanley Cups from 1976-79.

10. Bobby Orr, the Boston Bruin who revolutionized defensive play putting the accent on goal-scoring and play-making.

11. Maurice Richard, considered The Babe Ruth of hockey and the first player ever to score 50 goals in 50 games.

12. Frank Mahovlich, top gun on the Toronto Maple Leaf club that won Stanley Cups in 1962, 1963, 1964 and 1967.

The Three Most Relevant Contemporary Hockey People Whose Names Begin with the Letter G

1. *Bob Goodenow.* Ever since he became executive director of the National Hockey League Players' Association, the average salary has climbed from $300,000 to $600,000. Admired by the players, Goodenow is one of the most powerful people in the game.

2. *Wayne Gretzky.* Although his best years are long past, The Great One now has important off-ice power with the Los

Angeles Kings and remains the most visible player in the world — and most marketable.

3. *Jim Gregory.* In the Gary Bettman-led NHL, which is now dominated more and more by non-hockey business types, Gregory is the second most powerful hockey person, after vice-president Brian Burke.

THE TEN BEST FIGHTERS OF THE PAST DECADE

1. *Bob Probert.* He fought more and won more than anyone. Overall, the most feared player of the 1984-1994 period.

2. *Dave Brown.* The Incredible Hulk from Broad Street was not so much a bully as he was an authentic enforcer who, in retrospect, did right in beating up on Tomas Sandstrom.

3. *Marty McSorley.* Granted, he lost a few here and there, but few policemen fought more, got paid more and played more than Smilin' Marty.

4. *Joe Kocur.* Until his knuckles simply wore out from wear and tear, this Mean Machine was the equal of the best punchers in the league. At times, he even topped Probert.

5. *Tie Domi.* Pound for pound, The Albanian Assassin was the most courageous to leap over the boards. Ask Probert who had his hands full with Tie more than once.

6. *Craig Berube.* A solid citizen who could play the game as well as slug, Berube has obtained far less credit for his effective fisticuffs than he deserved. He was the first to go even with then-undefeated heavyweight Troy Crowder.

7. *Rick Tocchet.* Unquestionably the most talented tough guy of the decade, Tocchet climbed from the goon category to goal-scorer, but he never forgot how to toss an uppercut.

8. *Tony Twist.* There have been precious few players who thoroughly enjoy throwing punches than The Twister. He's almost professorial about his role and holds the unofficial NHL speed record for lefts and rights.

9. *Ken Daneyeko.* The NHL's iron man for several years, Dano ranks among the strongest belters of the modern era. He has a special knack for avoiding enemy blows.

Worst position to be in while still coming out a winner. The NHL's best fighter of his era, John Ferguson (left) appears ready to KO Bob Nevin of the Rangers. Interestingly, Nevin blocked the blow and fought Fergie to a draw, which was like a victory.

10. *Wendel Clark.* He's a mean maverick who makes up in intensity what he may lack in size. His jabs are rapid fire with the knack of getting inside his foe.

The Record for Home Games Played on the Road by a Pro Team

From January until April 1993, the St. John's Maple Leafs of the American Hockey League were forced out of their home arena because of a strike by city workers. For four months, the Leafs had to play their home games out of a suitcase, playing in every province east of Manitoba. These included:

1. Toronto
2. Cornwall
3. Hamilton
4. Montreal
5. Saint John (New Brunswick)
6. Charlottetown
7. Stephenville (Newfoundland)
8. Halifax

"It was an incredible learning experience," said Leafs coach Joel Quenneville, "but it was tough on girlfriends, wives and kids."

Best NHL Play-by-Play Man as Thespian

Gene Hart, who has been the broadcaster for the Philadelphia Flyers since the team's inception in 1967, made his debut with the Bohème Opera Company in Trenton, New Jersey in 1993. Gene made his maiden appearance as Frosch, the drunken jailer, in Strauss' "Die Fledermaus". Hart also has appeared with the famed Philadelphia Orchestra as the narrator in Aaron Copeland's "Lincoln Portrait." Hart observes, "Now I only need ballet for my artistic hat trick."

The Two Worst NHL Roof Collapses

1. *Philadelphia, 1968.* During the Flyers' first big-league campaign, 1967-68, The Broad Street skaters played out of the brand-new Spectrum. However, a late-season storm tore a huge hole in the roof, forcing cancellation of games through the homestretch. Without home ice, the Flyers were forced to play "home" games on foreign rinks such as Madison Square Garden and Le Colisée in Quebec. Despite such adversity, Philadelphia finished in first place in the NHL's West Division.

2. *Hartford, 1978.* A heavy snowstorm left an unnatural layer of white stuff on the roof of the Civic Center. Under the weight of the snow, the 1,400-ton lattice-type space-frame roof that spanned 2 1/2 acres collapsed. Ironically, Howard Baldwin, who had worked for the Flyers in 1968, was president of the Whalers when the cave-in took place. Said Baldwin, "The roof problem in Philly was just a few shingles falling off compared to the Hartford collapse. It was unbelievable; devastating." The Whalers switched their home games to the Springfield Civic Center until the roof repairs were finished on February 6, 1980.

Best One-Eyed Personalities

1. *Bill Chadwick.* One of the most respected referees in NHL history, Chadwick spent 16 years in the bigs, although he was blind in his right eye. Chadwick eventually made his way to the Hockey Hall of Fame.

2. *Glen Sonmor.* A New York Rangers prospect, the left wing lost his sight after the l954-55 season but remained active in hockey as coach and manager for many years.

3. *Tommy Burlington.* Had there been a 26-team NHL today, this excellent forward certainly would have been a better-than-average player. As it happened, he was confined to the American League, starring for the Cleveland Barons, although he had sight out of only one eye.

Most Embarrassing Debut for a Hockey Team

When the World Hockey Association opened its first season, 1967-68, a team was placed in Philadelphia to compete with the Flyers. Instead of playing at The Spectrum, the WHA's Blazers were housed in Convention Hall, which supposedly had been refurbished to mint condition for the premiere game between the New England Whalers and the Blazers. As the rink filled to capacity, the Zamboni machine rolled out for a last resurfacing. However, as it began its rounds, the ice collapsed under the machine forcing postponement of the game. Blazers star Derek Sanderson addressed the audience, trying to soothe the irate fans, but was pelted with orange pucks handed out as souvenirs.

Five Reasons Why Gil Stein Had the Shortest Term of any National Hockey League President

1. His attitude — progressive in the eyes of some — angered several owners who decided they wanted another personality type.

2. His punitive policy of suspending players for non-game days was ridiculed by the media and fans.

3. His summer 1992 cross-continent tour had too many believing that he was campaigning for himself, not the NHL.

4. League governors wanted someone who was an expert in marketing. Stein's expertise was in the legal end.

5. He was considered too old for the job.

The Greatest Line Not in the NHL

Those who had the good fortune to have seen The Hot Line — Bobby Hull-Ulf Nilsson-Anders Hedberg — in action from the fall of 1974 to the spring of 1978 will attest that they were as sensational as any hockey trio seen anywhere, anytime. United with the Winnipeg Jets, they marauded through the World Hockey Association as well as The Punch Line or Production Line did in the NHL. Actually, they came together almost by accident during a workout before the 1974-75 season. "I was standing in one corner and Ulf and Anders were in the other," Hull remembered. "I took off up my wing.

The next thing I know they were coming out like rockets. It was bing-bing-bing. Five passes later, the puck was resting in the net. 'Holy smoke,' I said to myself. 'Are these guys real?'"

By the time they were through, The Hot Line had paced the Jets to two WHA titles (1975-76 and 1977-78) and a near-miss of a third (1976-77) while totalling 573 goals and 804 assists for 1,377 points over four seasons."It was as good a line as I've ever seen," concluded Glen Sonmor who coached

When it came to quickest rise and most abrupt fall from glory, Jack McCarten shares that distinction with Jim Craig, both goalies on Gold Medal Olympic squads. McCarten (seen here in Rangers regalia) starred on Uncle Sam's 1960 championship squad at Squaw Valley, but didn't last very long in the bigs. Ditto for Craig, hero of the 1980 Lake Placid winners, who exited after a very short NHL stint.

the WHA's Birmingham Bulls. "Other great lines that have been put together had a scorer, a grinder and a playmaker. They didn't need a grinder."

Best Putdown of a Wayne Gretzky-Owned Automobile

After The Great One's wife, Janet Jones, bought her husband a new Ferrari, valued at $200,000, Oilers forward Kelly Buchburger declared, "His car is worth more than I make — in fact, it's worth more than my house!"

Top Six Players Playoff Teams Can't Afford to Lose

1. *Mark Messier-Rangers:* If Messier goes down, the Rangers' goose is cooked. Messier is the Rangers' only play-making center and undisputed leader of the team. Sure, Adam Graves and Kevin Lowe can step into the leadership role, but a Messier-void in the middle can not be filled.

2. *Patrick Roy-Canadiens*: The Conn Smythe Trophy winner last year means more to his team than any other goaltender. The 1993 champs are only average without Patrick between the pipes. The acquisition of Ron Tugnutt strengthens the No. 2 spot considerably, but if the Canadiens have to rely on Tugnutt the chances for a second straight are slim.

3. *Curtis Joseph-Blues:* If Roy is the most relied upon goalie than Cujo is a close second. Nobody faces more rubber

than Joseph on the defense-weak Blues. Jim Hrivnak has only played in a handful of games and has not overly impressed. A Joseph-less Blues squad wouldn't win a game in the playoffs, no matter how much Ron Caron pays his Peter's, Nedved and Stastny.

4. *Jeremy Roenick-Blackhawks:* Even with Roenick, the Hawks won't go far this post-season. Without him the closest Chicago would get to the playoffs is a bar-side stool at their favorite Rush Street pub. Roenick is the Hawks only threat on offense and if he doesn't play spectacular hockey, the Hawks don't win.

5. *Pavel Bure-Canucks:* Bure is to the Canucks what Teemu Selanne was to the Jets. Maybe Vancouver wouldn't fall quite as far as the Jets did but they would be struggling for a playoff spot without him. Bure is the only gifted offensive player on the Canucks and they need speed to take the pressure off a slow and immobile defense.

6. *Dale Hawerchuk-Sabres:* Ducky is playing his best hockey in years. Alex Mogilny may be wearing the captain's "C" but don't let that fool you; Hawerchuk is as much the leader as Mogilny. Without Pat LaFontaine, Hawerchuk assumed the top spot in the middle and has led the team to the top of the league.

Top Five Power Forwards

1. *Cam Neely-Bruins:* Neely is having the best season of his career just when it was questionable whether he would even be able to play. He is a tree in front of the net and nobody takes more abuse in that spot. Neely is impossi-

ble to knock off the puck when it's on his stick and has a soft touch around the crease.

2. *Brendan Shanahan-Blues:* Last year was a breakthrough season for Brendan and he has done little to disappoint this year. He doesn't fight as much as past years but don't dare ruffle his feathers. Shanahan is on pace for a 50 goal, 50 assist, 200-penalty-minute season.

3. *Adam Graves-Rangers:* Graves has emerged from his role as Mark Messier's bodyguard to the complete hockey player. He's one of the best NHL hitters and plays in all situations (power play and penalty killing). When he breaks the Ranger record of 50 goals by Vic Hadfield, expect the roar from the Garden faithful to raise the roof.

4. *Kevin Stevens-Penguins:* Coming off the terrifying facial injury in Game Seven of the Patrick Division Finals Stevens resumed his intimidating style. He's back to where he was in the seasons past and should come close to the 50-goal mark for the third straight time in his career.

5. *Keith Tkachuk-Jets:* The 21-year-old Winnipeg captain has quickly become one of the NHL's most feared hitters. Hitting was never in doubt with Tkachuk. What came as a surprise to NHL observers was his ability to put points on the board. In only his second full season with the Jets, Keith finished with 40 goals, 40 assists, and close to 200 penalty minutes.

BEST FRANCHISE PLAYERS AT EACH POSITION

1. *C-Eric Lindros-Flyers*: A no-brainer. Eric has it all: size, speed and skill. His critics tend to forget this hulking

superstar is only 21 years old and when he matures he will be a combination of Mario Lemieux and Cam Neely.

2. *G-Felix Potvin-Maple Leafs:* Every great team needs a top notch goalie and Felix the Cat is the best young netminder in the game. At 22, Potvin is ready to take the torch from Patrick Roy and become the next French super goalie.

3. *D-Brian Leetch-Rangers:* The 26 year-old Leetch has still not yet reached his prime and already has a 100-point season and a Norris Trophy under his belt. Leetch has improved his defensive play this season under Mike Keenan and still is the most skilled offensive defenseman in the league.

4. *RW-Jaromir Jagr-Penguins:* The Czech sensation was drafted fifth overall in 1990. If it was done over again there is no doubt JJ would be first. When Jagr gets the puck, fans sit on the edge of their seats and goalies shake in their skates. Jagr came into his own when Mario went down in the '91-'92 playoffs and is on pace for his first 100-point season.

5. *D-Chris Pronger-Whalers:* More then one NHL general manager was overheard at last summer's draft saying that Pronger was either better than Alexandre Daigle or, the best defenseman drafted in the last 10 years. The next Larry Robinson is only 18 and will lead the Whalers into the next century.

6. *LW-Adam Graves-Rangers:* The captain of the team. Graves is a 30-goal scorer who will get 50 on hard work. The oldest forward on the list at 26, Graves would be the leader of this team on the ice, but more importantly in the dressing room.

Three Gutsy Moves by Injured Players

1. *Baun Scores Cup-Winner on Broken Foot.* In Game Six of the Stanley Cup finals between the Detroit Red Wings and the Toronto Maple Leafs, the latter club faced elimination, being down three games to two. Toronto coach Punch Imlach had relied on his rugged defenseman Bob Baun to deliver the most crunching bodychecks behind the Leafs' blue line, but Baun stopped a puck with his ankle and had to leave for repairs. Medics discovered that he had a broken bone, but Bob urged the doctor to shoot him with painkiller so that he could finish the game. They obliged and Baun returned to the lineup, taking his regular turn. In sudden-death overtime, he shot the game-winning goal, sending the series to a seventh game which his Toronto club won.

2. *Boom Boom Won't Be Daunted*: During the 1961 playoffs, the Montreal Canadiens were shooting for a sixth straight Stanley Cup. However, the Chicago Blackhawks were putting up mighty resistance. The Habs star was right wing Bernie "Boom Boom" Geoffrion, who had won the NHL scoring championship, tied Maurice Richard's 50-goal record and led the Canadiens to first place. But now the breaks were going against him. A serious knee injury apparently would sideline him for the rest of the spring. As the train speeding the Habs to Chicago for the sixth game moved through the night, Geoffrion studied the heavy plaster cast imprisoning his injured knee and then called captain Doug Harvey. "Look, Doug," he said, "one more loss and we're out. Let's cut the cast." Harvey borrowed a knife and they slipped into a washroom where they delicately removed the hard plaster. Geoffrion's knee was blotched with red. "It hurt so much I couldn't sleep,"

Geoffrion later recalled. "But I wanted to play. Next morning I asked coach Toe Blake to let me take a turn. At game time, Geoffrion's leg was frozen with painkiller. On his first turn, Bobby Hull and Reg Fleming of Chicago crashed Geoffrion to the ice; he tried to get up but collapsed as if his knee was stuffed with cardboard. Later, he attempted again to play but the knee was useless. Without Geoffrion, Montreal lost the game and missed the Stanley Cup finals for the first time in 11 years.

Bernie "Boom Boom" Geoffrion is listed among the gutsiest NHL players, but he also is notable for popularizing the slapshot in modern hockey. The Boomer was the first to try anything other than the wrist or backhander on a regular basis, beginning in the early 1950s. It wasn't until a decade later that other players picked up on the slapshot as a weapon.

3. *Battered Moore Wins Scoring Title.* Early in his career Dickie Moore, the nonpareil Montreal Canadiens left wing, suffered three shoulder separations, broken right knuckles and knee trouble. But in the 1957-58 season, he

displayed courage and competence above and beyond the call of duty. During that campaign, Moore was challenged for the scoring championship by teammate Henri Richard and Andy Bathgate of the New York Rangers. But with three months left in the season, Moore broke his left wrist and the title seemed beyond his grasp. "How about putting a cast on my arm," Moore suggested. "Let me take care of the rest." Sure enough, when the Canadiens faced off in their next game, there was Moore on the ice, handcuffed by a bulky plaster cast on his left arm. Gone was the freedom to stickhandle and the ease of flicking a wrist shot, but nothing dampened Dickie's spirit. He played in every game and scored 36 goals — tops in the league — with 48 assists, a total of 84 points. And Dickie had spent most of the season playing right wing — an unfamiliar position for him. P.S. A season later he was shifted back to left wing and, this time, he won his second scoring title, beating Gordie Howe's 1952-53 scoring record of 95 by one point!

The Absolutely Worst Use of a Curved Stick in Playoff Annals

During the 1993 Stanley Cup finals between the Montreal Canadiens and the Los Angeles Kings, the underdog Californians took a one-game lead into Game Two, and it appeared they were about to defeat the Habs at The Forum. Many critics believe that had Los Angeles taken a two-game lead back to the West Coast, Wayne Gretzky's club would have won the first Stanley Cup in the franchise's history. Sure enough, in the fading minutes of the third period, the Kings nursed a one-goal lead and appeared a shoo-in to beat Montreal. At that point, Canadiens coach Jacques Demers called for time and asked referee Kerry Fraser to have defenseman Marty McSorley's stick measured. Fraser brought the stick to NHL off-ice official Jeff Weintraub who produced his standard measuring device. The stick's curve was illegally drastic and the King was dispatched to the penalty box. Fortified with the extra skater, the Habs put the tying goal behind goalie Kelly Hrudey and won the game in overtime. From that point on, Montreal won three straight games and the Stanley Cup. Since then, McSorley has been more diligent about his stick curves.

Most Interesting U-Turn on a Hockey Autobiography

When Brett Hull completed his life story — up through 1992 — the publisher, Prentice-Hall of Canada, wanted to title it *Hot Shot*, because The Golden Brett was a hot hockey player and he packed a smoldering shot. But Hull's advisors feared that such a label would make him appear to egocentric. When the book finally was published, it was called, *Shootin' and Smilin'*.

The Six Best Conachers in Hockey

1. *Charlie Conacher.* A member of the Hockey Hall of Fame, Charlie was right wing on Toronto's famed Kid Line along with Busher Jackson and Joe Primeau. He was twice the NHL's leading scorer (1934, 1935) and three-time First All-Star. During the early 1930s, Charlie was considered the hardest shooter in the game.

2. *Roy Conacher.* Kid brother of Charlie, Roy ranks among the most underrated of the clan. He was an ace left wing with Boston, Detroit and Chicago, and was the NHL's leading scorer in 1949, as well as First Team All-Star. Roy, who had a very accurate shot, broke into the NHL in 1938 and finished his career in 1952.

3. *Lionel Conacher.* Nicknamed "The Big Train," Lionel was voted Canada's Athlete of the Half-Century (1900-1950) for his exploits on ice as well as the football field. A defenseman, he launched his NHL career with the Pittsburgh Pirates in 1925 but hit the heights in Montreal with the Maroons. He was First Team All-Star in 1934 and concluded his career in 1937, after stints with the New York Americans and Chicago Blackhawks.

4. *Brian Conacher.* Last of the famed Conacher family to skate in the majors, Brian turned regular with the Toronto Maple Leafs in the 1966-67 season, and was a major factor in Punch Imlach's march to the Stanley Cup that year. Brian concluded his career in 1972 with Ottawa Nationals of the World Hockey Association, after skating briefly for the Detroit Red Wings.

5. *Pete Conacher.* The son of Charlie, Pete was an athlete with too many press clippings to carry (mostly his dad's). Pete made his debut in 1951-52 playing two games for the Blackhawks. He was dealt to the New York Rangers in November 1954 and finished his NHL career on Broadway in 1956.

6. *Pat Conacher.* Unrelated to any of the other Conachers, this honest workman spanned 15 NHL seasons, from 1979 to 1994. He started with the Rangers and played for the

Stanley Cup-winning Oilers as well as the New Jersey Devils and the Los Angeles Kings, who reached the Cup finals with Pat in 1993. Ironically, his nickname is Charlie.

MOST UNUSUAL PROBE OF A HOCKEY FAN'S CAR

Robert Paskal, a lawyer, ranks among the most intense hockey fans of all time. According to the *St. Louis Post-Dispatch*, Paskal and his wife, Jake, moved from St. Louis to Boothbay Harbor, Maine, "in part because it put them closer to more levels of hockey action." Paskal had been a St. Louis Blues season ticket-holder from the 1967-68 season and a fan of the Central League's St. Louis Flyers and Braves before that. One story has it that Paskal once flew from St. Louis to Boston where he rented a car and drove to and from Moncton, New Brunswick. Reporter John McGuire related that he executed the 1,600 mile round-trip "just to see a minor-league game." It was when Paskal crossed the border at Calais, Maine that the trouble started. Canadian customs agents stopped Paskal and held him for three hours. "They tore his car apart looking for drugs," said reporter McGuire. "They even made him dump the coffe he had in his Thermos and wouldn't let him go to the bathroom." The customs agents couldn't believe that a hockey nut would take a trip from St. Louis to Moncton to see a small-town game. "They were certain the story I was telling them just couldn't be true," concluded Paskal. But Robert's friends knew better.

Most Unusual Place for a Hockey Fan to Propose Marriage

During the second and third periods of a game between Binghamton and Huntington of the East Coast Hockey League in 1993-94, a most unusual event unfolded on the ice of the Huntington, West Virginia rink. Christy Stubblefield actually believed she had won a ride on the Zamboni ice surfacing machine. But after one trip around the rink, her boyfriend, Alan Gianettino, stepped on the ice and handed her a bouquet of flowers. "Is this the last place you expected this to happen?" Gianettino asked before dropping to one knee. "Will you marry me, Christy?" She nodded her head with a huge smile. "I wanted to get off that thing," said Stubblefield. "It stopped and I saw Alan with the flowers and I thought, 'Isn't that nice.' I had no idea he was going to give me a ring."

Best Press Room Fight in Canada, 1993-94

Usually members of the media prefer describing hockey fights on the air or in print, but a couple of Montreal journalists did a first-person version of a fight at Montreal's Forum. Radio broadcasters Dino Sisto and Mitch Melnick went at it in the cramped Forum press room so intensely that ten security people were required to separate the warring pair. Neither was given a game misconduct, but they were barred from The Forum for two weeks.

Rocket Richard's Favorite Goal

"We were playing the Bruins in the 1952 playoffs and the series went down to the seventh and last game of the semi-finals. I was going around the defensemen or between them and Leo

Labine of the Bruins hit me just as I was falling to the ice. While I was down, he hit me on the head with his knee. I was cut open and knocked cold. They took me to The Forum clinic and woke me up, and I came back to the bench. I actually didn't know where I was or what team I was playing for and they probably could have sent me to the hospital, but I wanted to finish the game. Then, I went out on the ice and was dizzy. I didn't know which end was which. But don't you think I wound up scoring the winning goal? I hit the puck, didn't know what happened, and only found out afterwards because I saw a movie of it. But when it actually went in I wasn't too sure. My father came into the dressing room after the game and everybody said it was my best goal."

Maurice "Rocket" Richard easily wins the award for most intense eyes in NHL history. The Rocket engages in a staring contest here with Rangers defenseman Ivan "The Terrible" Irwin. As usual, Richard out-stared his foe.

Three Reasons Why Pat Burns Won't Win A Stanley Cup with the Leafs

1. Stresses too strong of a defensive style — he's not in Montreal any longer.

2. Patrick Roy is not on his team.

3. Wendel Clark's loss deprives his team of leadership.

Five Reasons Why Hockey Officiating Is the Worst of All Major Sports

1. No consistency — what was a penalty two minutes ago isn't now.

2. The officials think the fans are there to see them.

3. Anything goes in the last five minutes of the third period.

4. Linesmen can watch but not call a tripping penalty.

5. Two guys watching two lines, one guy watching the whole rink.

Hollywood's Best Hockey Movies

1. *KING OF HOCKEY:* Dick Purcell was the star of this melodrama in which the better-known Wayne Morris played a goalie named "Jumbo." Whenever the cameras zeroed in on Purcell, he was shown only from the waist

up. Obviously, Purcell couldn't skate worth a lick. It was filmed in 1936.

2. *IDOL OF THE CROWD:* The Duke himself, John Wayne, portrayed a sharp stickhandler in this opus made in 1937. Wayne may have been a great horseman and gunslinger, but he clearly wasn't much of a skater or shooter. Not once did the filmgoer ever see Duke skating. First a shot of his body and then cut to a pair of skating legs — indubitably those of a stunt man.

3. *HELL'S KITCHEN:* Ronald Reagan was a young star when the already popular Dead End Kids (Leo Gorcey, Huntz Hall, et al.) were big names in Hollywood. In this film, the Dead Enders wind up playing hockey for a reform school against what they mistakenly believe is another such institution. Too late, they discover that the other school substituted a bunch of professional hockey players. Unlike the John Wayne and Dick Purcell flicks, this one — made in 1939 — displayed a bit of authenticity, since members of the NHL's New York Americans were used for the hockey scene. Hockey historian Ira Gitler also notes: "There were shots of the Dead End Kids flying up on the boards, like gymnasts, and vaulting back into the play."

4. *IT'S A PLEASURE:* Released in 1945, this was a solid "B" movie starring Michael O'Shea which had as its main theme the promotion of a hockey star. Its significance lies in the fact that it was technically the best hockey film made to date.

5. *SUSPENSE:* Hockey was merely an incidental backdrop in this 1946 movie co-starring the ice queen, Belita, and veteran actor Barry Sullivan.

6. *THE FRIENDS OF EDDIE COYLE:* Robert Mitchum is the top name in a melodrama also featuring Peter Boyle. The latter plays a Bruins fan. A key scene takes place in Boston Garden while an actual NHL game is in progress. It was shot in 1973.

7. *THE APRIL FOOLS:* Catherine Deneuve and Jack Lemmon portray a pair of lovers who, at one point, camp in the empty stands at The Forum in Inglewood, California during a Los Angeles Kings scrimmage.

8. *LOVE STORY:* The film version of the best-selling novel offers Ryan O'Neal, playing hockey for Harvard, brawling with Boston College stickhandlers as a way of displaying his *machismo* to Ali McGraw.

9. *PAPERBACK HERO:* More authentic than most hockey flicks, this 1974 movie was filmed in the prairie hamlet of Delisle, Saskatchewan, home of Hall-of-Famers Max and Doug Bently.

10. *FACE-OFF:* Toronto Maple Leafs fans had a field day watching their heroes George Armstrong and Jim McKenny as well as then-Boston Bruin Derek Sanderson. The script has a hockey player falling in love with a rock singer. The movie was completed in 1971.

11. *HOCKEY HOMICIDE:* Walt Disney's cartoon favorite Goofy starred in this splendid short that, sadly, never seems to be shown on re-runs.

12. *SLAPSHOT:* In terms of production costs and overall hype, this Paul Newman extravaganza was the biggest (though not necessarily the best) hockey movie yet. To

hockey purists, it was awful. To those interested in a Hollywood comedy, it was sprinkled with laughs.

13. *YOUNGBLOOD:* This movie stars Rob Lowe as a young hockey player, who is playing Juniors in Western Canada. He goes through all the hardships of life as a hockey star — the initiation, the trials and acceptance of his teammates, his coaches and, most importantly, his father. He also falls in love with the girl who drives the Zamboni, who turns out to be the coach's daughter. She helps him through his rough times and never stops believing in him. The camera shows Rob Lowe playing hockey, but in the parts when he's on the ice alone practicing his skating or taking a penalty shot, the camera only shows him from the waist up or the legs down. Give it three stars.

14. *THE MIGHTY DUCKS:* Walt Disney's version of the Big Bad Sport. In this film, Emilio Estevez portrays an ex-hockey star turned cold-hearted lawyer. He is charged with driving while intoxicated and has to do community service. He is given a choice of either going to jail or coaching a pee-wee hockey team. He chooses the latter. The team turns out to be the worst team in the league, not to mention an odd bunch. Estevez teaches these kids how to play like a team and the meaning of friendship. In return, the kids teach him to be kind and caring. Eventually, he leads the team to the championships where they win it all. He then leaves to go play semi-pro hockey. How bad can it be? A real, live NHL team was a result of it.

15. *THE MIGHTY DUCKS II:* Most of the original cast return for the sequel. Emilio is having a great career in the semi-pros until a cheap shot to the knee lands him in the

stands. He goes back to Minnesota to recuperate and winds up coaching the US Junior Olympic Team. Most of the old team is together again with some new faces added to make the team incredible, although they need lots of practice before this happens. He is offered a job as spokesman for an equipment company but, as usual, gets caught up in the whole idea. Fortunately for the team, he comes back down to earth in time to win — along with the help of his friends — the gold for the US. This movie even has a guest appearance by The Great One, Wayne Gretzky. Unfortunately, completely out of character for Disney, it glorifies violence below and beyond the call of duty. Sorry, only one star for this dud.

THE ALL-TIME NON-NHL LOSERS

There have been bad hockey teams, dreadful hockey teams, subterranean clubs — and then there was the Princeton University varsity sextet, circa 1970-71.

Oddly enough, it was supposed to be a decent team, if not an Eastern College Athletic Conference champion. Any supporter of the Princeton Tigers that year had reason for hope. Behind the bench, the Ivy League club had a man of infinite wisdom. Bill Quackenbush had not only starred for Stanley Cup-winners in Detroit, but had also played capably for the Boston Bruins and was a member of the Hockey Hall of Fame. Such credentials, even by National Hockey League standards, were impeccable.

Quackenbush was not inheriting a brand-new team in a brand-new school. The Tigers have enjoyed a long and rich hockey heritage, and in 1970-71 a number of varsity veterans were returning to the club as well as a spate of Canadian-developed sophomores. Champions are made of such elements and there were nothing but positive signs in the training period before the start of regular play. Ed Swift, who wrote about the team in *Sports Illustrated*, observed: "The players looked forward eagerly to the opening game."

It was to be their last breath of optimism.

Before their Christmas respite had arrived — much too late, they felt — the Princetonians had lost six straight games. In his wildest nightmares Quackenbush couldn't have imagined such an opening. But there were 17 games remaining and — what the heck — teams have been known to stem a losing tide. Unfortunately, Wisconsin, the first foe following the Yale break, was not cooperative. The Badgers demolished the Tigers 9-0. Most extraordinary.

Not that Princeton never took a lead and looked like a winner. They were doing just fine against Clarkson, managing four goals to Clarkson's one late in the second period and, for once, appearing capable of victory. A fifth goal appeared on the horizon when the Tigers burst forth with a three-man breakaway. Not only did they have an opportunity for a clear shot but, even if the Clarkson goalie made the save, there was a chance at a rebound.

Except the Tigers went offside on the play.

Before Princeton could pull itself together, the foe scored twice. "Any team that puts itself offside on a three-man breakaway," said Princeton's goaltender, "is too stupid to beat Clarkson."

He was right. Princeton blew the lead and the game. Final score, 6-4 for Clarkson.

By now a tie would have been considered a moral victory, but ties didn't come easily either. Refusing to settle for a 5-5 tie, Brown edged Princeton, 6-5, on a flukey weak shot in the final seconds of the match. "I lost the puck in the black of an umbrella," the goalie explained.

A potential win against Army was squandered when an especially ardent anti-war activist on the Princeton club blew his cool against the Plebes and spent considerable time in the penalty box. The West Pointers scored five power-play goals and won, 7-2.

"Princeton entered a game with so little confidence," wrote Swift, "that it instilled a feeling in its foes that nothing could go wrong. Nothing ever did."

Such losers were the Princetonians that when two Tigers engaged in a practice fight, they both believed that they had lost. "It's possible for both participants to lose a fight," said Swift, "but I had never before heard of both *admitting* to being beaten."

Pretty soon, a 5-3 loss or a 6-4 defeat was close enough to be considered a victory, but there was no solace whatsoever to be obtained from such as the 14-0 loss to Boston University. At the end of the second period, Princeton's goalie fell asleep from exhaustion. When he was awakened to take the ice for the third period, the goalie sighed: "Maybe they'll start without me."

The 14-0 debacle marked Princeton's 11th straight loss but, at last, victory was to come. It required overtime to do it, but the Tigers defeated Colgate, 5-4, and one suspected good things were on the horizon. Or were they? "In a way," wrote Swift, "it was cruel to the players for them to win when they did. Coming at exactly the halfway point in the schedule, it gave Princeton just enough hope to last the rest of the year."

For the team members there was hardly time to savor the single victory. A story soon appeared in the school newspaper, *The Daily Princetonian*, with a blaring headline: "HOCKEY WIN NULLIFIED!" According to the dispatch, coach Bill Quackenbush allegedly was nabbed dispensing pep pills to his skaters. Although the story was obviously part of the *Princetonian*'s annual lampoon issue, as often happens a number of readers took it seriously.

Swift, who is now a staff writer for *Sports Illustrated*, played goal for that ill-fated Princeton sextet and he recalled in his story how his teammates frequently extolled the enemy, as if the enemy were their teammates. He mentioned how once, in a game against Cornell, a member of the Big Red skimmed a perfect pass between defenseman Peter D'Ewart's legs to a Cornell teammate, at which point D'Ewart shouted: "Nice pass" to the foe. "When D'Ewart returned to the bench," Swift recalled, "Quackenbush asked him dryly if he was enjoying the game. Peter nodded."

As the varsity goalie, Swift could appreciate how the fans remained loyal to the losers — they ran up yet another 11-game losing streak after their lone win — right to the very end. Even though their record was 1-21, Princeton sold out its final game at home, a match against Dartmouth. They lost that one, too, 4-3, and then one of the weirdest thind happened. Instead of leaving the ice in silence, the terrible Tigers received the kind of treatment usually reserved for champions — a two-minute ovation!

THE MOST TRADED MAN IN HOCKEY

The dream of most young boys growing up in the cold winters of Canada is to eventually play on a National Hockey League team. Depending on where they grow up, they may fantasize about the Canadiens, or perhaps imagine themselves skating up and down the ice for the Toronto Maple Leafs or the Detroit Red Wings. Eddie Shore fans might seen themselves sporting the jersey of the mighty Boston Bruins — the list goes on and on. But for one man, Larry Morley Hillman, the dream of playing in the National Hockey Leauge began to resemble a nightmare when he found himself playing for not only each of the teams listed above, but a host of other NHL, AHL and WHA clubs during his 20-years-plus career. Larry Hillman, known to teammates, coaches and managers, and trainers alike as "Morley," is holder of the dubious honor of being the most traded man in hockey.

Born in Kirkland Lake, Ontario, in February of 1937, Larry Hillman shared the dream of his fellow youngsters, to someday make the National Hockey League. Being of limited natural talent but large size, he was relegated to the duties of defenseman. With hard work and determination, he cracked the NHL in the middle of the 1954-55 season after two and a half years in Junior "A" with Hamilton and Windsor. Ironically, or perhaps more ominously, Hillman didn't even complete his Junior career with one team, as most juniors do; rather, he moved from Windsor (after one year there) to the Hamilton Tiger-Cubs where he played a year and a half before turning pro with the Detroit Red Wings.

Towards the end of the 1954-55 season, Hillman signed a Jack Adams-Detroit Red Wings contract, played in six games in the Motor City, and was part of the roster when the Red Wings, powered by Lindsay, Howe, Delvecchio and Sawchuk, won the Stanley Cup for the second year in a row by defeating the Montreal Canadiens in a dramatic seven-game series. Morley spent the next two seasons (1955-56 and 1956-57) between Detroit and the American League Buffalo Bisons, and Detroit and the Western League Edmonton Flyers.

Still, the image of the hard, back-breaking work in the gold mines of Kirkland Lake was inspiration enough for Hillman to continue to dedicate himself to the game he loved so much. In the summer of 1957, Hillman was drafted from the Red Wings by the Chicago Blackhawks. He never even put on the jersey. Just hours before the start of the 1957-58 season, the Boston Bruins pecked him off the Chicago roster and assigned him to full duty. That season, Larry Hillman appeared in 70 games for the Bruins, exceeding the number of games he played for Detroit in three seasons by one. Morley continued his steady play through the 1958-59 season while appearing in only 55 games. In 1959-60, Hillman was rewarded for his dedication and perserverence with a ticket to the Providence Reds of the Amercian Hockey League. Morley really showed 'em, though. He won the Eddie Shore Award as the league's top rearguard, was selected for the AHL First All-Star Team, and to top it off, got a bus ride to Toronto, courtesy of the intra-league draft. At the age of 23, after over five seasons as a pro, Larry Hillman was once more packing his bags, this time going to his fourth NHL team.

By now two forces were at work in the back of Morley's mind — first of all that nobody seemed to want him, and secondly everybody was trading *for* him. He had earned respectability among his teammates and throughout the managerial level of most of the NHL clubs through his steady, unflashy, hard-working style of play. Still, he couldn't seem to find himself a permanent spot on any club in the big leagues, though after his blue ribbon performance in Providence, the Toronto Maple Leafs were high enough on him to draft him away from the Bruins organization.

Returning to Ontario initially presented itself as a dream come true, but the pattern of the past was fated to haunt Hillman throughout his eight seasons in Toronto. Punch Imlach, who saw duty as both general manager and coach, gave Morley an opportunity in his first season as a Leaf, playing him in 62 games. He was then shipped to the minors, this time the AHL Rochester Americans. From 1961 until his eventual (inevitable) departure from the Toronto organization in 1968, Hillman yo-yoed back and forth from Toronto to Rochester, with one detour in 1962-63 when he spent the large part of a hellish year with Eddie Shore and his Indians of Springfield, Massachusetts.

At the age of 31, following eight torturously frustrating years with Toronto, and accumulating four more Stanley Cup rings (plus one with Detroit equalled five), Hillman became property of New York, and then later that day, the Minnesota

North Stars. On a bright sunny June morning in 1968 Larry Hillman received a call from North Stars' GM Wren Blair, who had phoned to congratulate Hillman on becoming a North Star. Hillman was growing more and more wary of ringing telephones and knocks on the door. He was getting set to join his eleventh professional team in 14 seasons, an unprecedented (and undesirable) amount of travelling for even the most extreme "journeymen" of the game.

The Worst Team Ever

There has been some speculation as to which hockey club deserves the dubious distinction of being called "The Worst Team Ever." Some Washingtonians will argue that the Caps of 1976-77 ranks as the most abysmal sextet on ice. Residents of Nassau and Suffolk (New York) counties will point a finger at the 1972-73 Islanders. But there was one club even worse. Prior to the start of the 1928-29 National Hockey League season, Benny Leonard, who had been the lightweight champion of the world, bought the NHL's Pittsburgh franchise and operated it in the Smoky City as The Pirates with no financial success.

On October 18, 1930, the NHL Board of Governors approved Leonard's request to move the Pittsburgh franchise to Philadelphia. Ebullient Benny reacted as if he had been granted a license to coin money. He promptly spelled out elaborate plans for the "new" club, renamed The Quakers, and promised Philadelphians a brand new ice palace, which would replace the already antiquated Arena. Within one season Leonard's Quakers would set new records of abject mediocrity. But, for the moment, Leonard could only see a fortune on the horizon.

"The present building won't be large enough to hold the crowds," Benny boasted. "We are expecting a larger one to be erected three years from now. If it isn't, I intend to bring New York capital in here and erect a modified Madison Square Garden that will house hockey, six-day bicycle races and wrestling."

Leonard's transplanted Pittsburgh club was nothing to crow about, either artistically or financially. As for The Pirates, they finished dead last in the American Division of the NHL during the 1929-30 campaign. Their record of five wins, 36 losses, and three ties was generally regarded as the joke of the NHL — and it was hardly surprising that one of the leading jokesters on the Pirates was their goaltender — Joe Miller.

Miller accompanied Leonard to Philadelphia but Benny's optimism was not diminished one iota. "I think ice hockey has the greatest future of any sport in America," Leonard predicted. "So I'm willing to risk my money. I've lost plenty so far but I'm not crying. It's the coming sport in Philadelphia and two years from now you'll say I was right."

Leonard's choice as general manager-coach of the Quakers was Cooper Smeaton, a widely respected hockey man who had been referee-in-chief of the NHL at the time of his appointment. Smeaton had been through the hockey wars and was thankful to be alive when Leonard phoned him about the job. Being a referee was not a very safe job in those "frontier" days of pro hockey.

Smeaton had survived a number of close calls. Once, while officiating a match between Ottawa and Quebec in Quebec City, Cooper called several plays against the home club which enraged the already hostile French-Canadian audience.

Ottawa won the game by one goal and Smeaton was generally considered the culprit by the audience, a fact of which the referee was acutely aware. "Lucky for me," said Smeaton, "the referee and linesmen used to share the visiting team's dressing room since we didn't have a changing room of our own. I realized how fortunate I was moments after the final buzzer that night in Quebec."

The hard-nosed, outspoken Smeaton was Leonard's kind of man and served to stoke up more of Benny's enthusiastic fire. "This is a major league operation," Leonard boasted prior to the Quakers' opening game. "The Quakers are to ice hockey what the Athletics (then world champions) are to baseball."

Leonard was half right. He did have a major league operation everywhere but on the ice. His trainer, Archie Campbell, was as big-league as general manager-coach Smeaton. Campbell, after returning from service in World War I, worked for a good many hockey and football teams.

Campbell had been around sports operations a lot longer than Leonard. One look at the Quakers roster and Archie saw the handwriting on the wall. "Benny knew his hockey," said Campbell, "but I could tell, as far as that team was concerned, he didn't have a chance."

Plain and simple, the Quakers didn't have the talent. Forwards Hibbert "Hib" Milks and Gerald Lowrey were the best of a mediocre lot. Dubious about Joe Miller's goaltending capabilities, Smeaton also signed 21-year-old Welsh-born Wilf Cude. A high-strung personality, Cude spent a horrendous season guarding the Quakers goal. The experience, no doubt, brought on Cude's premature retirement from the sport in what is regarded as one of the most unusual retirement episodes in the game.

"I was having my afternoon steak before a game," said Cude, "and I poured a helluva lot of catsup on it. I'd just started to eat the steak when my wife, Beulah, made some casual remark about a trivial subject. For no good reason I picked up my steak and threw it.

"The steak wound up smacking against the wall. The catsup splattered and the steak hung there on the wall. Slowly it began to slip down and I stared at it. Between the time that steak hit the wall and then hit the floor, I decided I'd had enough of goaltending. When it landed I had made my decision to retire."

Judging by the Quakers' record in their first weeks of operation, one could understand Cude's edginess, not to mention Smeaton's. Philadelphia opened the 1930-31 season at the Arena on November 11, 1930, and lost 3-0 to the New York Rangers. They scored only one goal in the first three games, all losing affairs, before tying Ottawa 2-2. A momentous occasion — the Quakers first victory — took place on November 25, 1930, at the Arena. The Toronto Maple Leafs were beaten, 2-1.

Leonard began to get the message but his enthusiasm still ran high. "We're off to a slow start here this year," he admitted, "but I'm positive that Philadelphians will take to major hockey in another year or two. They have to become educated to it."

Leonard underestimated the Philadelphia fans. They were quite educated and were quick to realize that Benny had assembled what was to become the worst team in big-league hockey history. They did not win a single game from November 29, 1930, to January 10, 1931, and set a league record which still stands, losing 15 consecutive matches.

Somewhat depressed by now but still hopeful, Leonard made a few trades and imported Stan Crossett, a towering defenseman from Port Hope, Ontario. Crossett's experience in the NHL — and one episode in particular — symbolized more than anything the ill-starred life of the Quakers.

The Quakers were in Detroit for a game against the Falcons (later the Red Wings) and Smeaton gathered his men together for a pre-game skull session. He addressed himself mainly to Crossett, warning him against trying to split the vaunted Detroit defense of Reg Noble and Harvey "Rocky" Rockburn.

"These two guys have perfected the art of sandwiching attackers," said Smeaton. "Noble steers people into Rockburn and then Rockburn creams you. If you try to split them you can get hurt. And I mean hurt!"

Crossett appeared to be listening, but then in the second period Crossett stole the puck from a Detroit skater and did precisely what Smeaton had told him not to do. Archie Campbell, the Quakers trainer, watched the play in awe from the Philadelphia bench.

"Noble got him first," Campbell remembered, "then Rockburn sent him flying off his feet. It was no ordinary hoist either. The big fellow seemed to take off like an airplane. Then he made a perfect three-point landing on elbows and stomach and starte to skid along the ice. The wind had probably been knocked out of him before he ever touched the ice."

Nobody helped the Quakers as much as goalie Cude, who played spectacularly in the Philadelphia nets after his rather shaky start. Wilf's problem was that he was new to the NHL and consequently unfamiliar with the big guns on the opposition. Soon after he took over the goaltending job from Joe Miller, Cude went up against the mighty Montreal Maroons.

Coach Smeaton realized that his young goaler needed some special advice about the Montreal sharpshooters, particularly after Wilf's busy first period against the Maroons. So between the first and second periods, Smeaton warned that the Quakers to keep an eye on the "Big S" line of Nels Stewart, Hooley Smith and Babe Siebert.

"Don't let that big lug Stewart stand too near our goal crease," warned Smeaton. "They don't call him 'Ole Poison' for nothing."

Edgy over the lecture, Cude broke in: "The hell with Stewart! I want my defense to keep an eye on that fellow wearing a cap. He's the one causing all my trouble."

The heretofore subdued Quakers dressing room suddenly erupted with laughter, all except the befuddled Cude. Finally, coach Smeaton, wearing a big grin, leaned toward this netminder and whispered: "Wilfie, my boy, the chap with the cap is Nels Stewart."

Benny Leonard was quite willing to tolerate such shenanigans as long as his team put up a good fight — and that they did even though frequently undermanned.

On Chrismas Day 1930, they pleased Benny to no end while at the same time losing 8-0 to the Bruins at Boston Garden. The Quakers and Bruins indulged in a Pier Six free-for-all which began when Hib Milks was heavily checked by George Owen of Boston.

Nearly every player from both teams participated in the brawl with one notable exception — goalie Cude. This was as good a tie as any for Wilfie to take a brief sabbatical from his trying job. And what Wilf saw from his vantage point in the crease was astonishing by any hockey fight standards.

"Even the officials took a couple on the chin before it was over," wrote Charles Coleman in *The Trail of the Stanley Cup*. "As the referees seemed to be making very little headway in suppressing the fight, the police were called in. Only two constables went over the board at first and they looked plaintively back for aid as they approached the melee. They were eventually joined by reinforcements."

After what seemed like hours of flailing sticks, crunching punches, and continuous bloodletting, th fighting eventually subsided. Referee Mickey Ion assessed major penalties with $15 fines to Owen, Eddie Shore, and Dit Clapper of the Bruins and to Milks, D'Arcy Coulson, and Allan Shields of Philadelphia.

From the Quakers' viewpoint, Clapper was the major culprit. He not only scored a three-goal hat trick against Cude but also knocked out Wally Kilrea of Philadelphia with a right cross to the chin.

A month later the Quackers showed their class, returning to Boston Garden for the first time since the 8-0 debacle. This time, goalie Cude looked like an Indian rubber man, contorting himself successfully well to help the Quakers to an 3-3 tie. It was a remarkable performance in that it even earned a line in the official NHL history. Cude followed that with a pair of wins over Detroit but it was too little, too late to save the Quakers.

The NHL Governors realized the depth of the Quakers' financial problems late in the season when the Montreal Canadiens decided to release defenseman Bert McCaffrey who surely would have helped the Philadelphia blue line corps. The waiver price was a mere $5000 and it was anticipated that Leonard would grab at the opportunity to bolster his team with an eye toward the next season. Instead, Leonard declined. Philadelphia had reached the bottom of the barrel.

Gallantly, if not gloriously, the Quakers completed their one and only season of NHL play on March 21, 1931, at the Forum in Montreal. Their opponents were a Montreal Canadiens team paced by Howie Morenz. Instead of a lackadaisically playing out the string, the Quakers battled the Montrealers as if it were the final game for the Stanley Cup.

Matching the Canadiens goal for goal — the final score was 4-4 — Philadelphia had the Forum crowd on their side, which stimulated the Montreals to even more determined efforts. On one of his spectacular rushes down the ice, Morenz dispatched a mighty slapshot at the Quakers' net. Claude lost sight of the rubber.

Before he could lift his glove to deflect the puck, it smashed against his jaw and sent him reeling backwards into the net while blood splattered scross the goal crease. Cude was carried from the ice, suffering a torn jaw which requried heavy stitching. Hugh McCormack, a former London, Ontario, goaltender-turned-sportswriter, then put on the pads and preserved the 4-4 tie.

Rather than departing the NHL in a blaze of glory, the Quakers made their exit in a pool of red ink. On September 26, 1931, NHL president Frank Calder made it official that Philadelphia had agreed to suspend its franchise for one year.

Players belonging to the Quakers were distributed among the clubs which finished lowest in the league. One of them, left winger Syd Howe — no relation to Gordie — was signed by Toronto and later dealt to Ottawa and St. Louis before landing in Detroit with the Red Wings. He was the only member of the Philadelphia sextet to gain permanent eminence. In June 1965, Howe was elected to the Hockey Hall of Fame. The others are just a vague memory to those who watched one of sport's most pathetic teams in action.

One of the earliest shots of Montreal Canadiens' star Dider Pitre. Note the logo — this shot was taken before the team had settled on their famous Club de Hockey Canadien logo.

Before they became the Maple Leafs, Toronto's NHL representative was the St. Patricks. The club's most glamourous star was Cecil "Babe" Dye.

Oh, brother! Phil Esposito is parked in his characteristic spot — the opposing team's crease. On this occasion he tries to bat the puck in against his younger brother, Tony.